Classic Country Style

CLASSIC COUNTRY STYLE
And How to Achieve It

MARY TREWBY

Introduction by

JOCASTA INNES

A BULFINCH PRESS BOOK

LITTLE, BROWN AND COMPANY

BOSTON   TORONTO   LONDON

Copyright © 1990 by
Conran Octopus Limited

First U.S. Paperback Edition 1993
Fourth printing, 1996
First published in Great Britain
by Conran Octopus Limited.

Typeset by Litho Link Ltd.,
Welshpool, Powys, UK.

Library of Congress Cataloging-
in-Publication Data
Trewby, Mary.
    Classic country style: and how
    to achieve it / Mary Trewby,
    introduction by Jocasta Innes.
    — 1st U.S. *ed.*
        p.   cm.
    "A Bulfinch Press book."
    Includes index.
    ISBN 0-8212-1828-X (hc)
    ISBN 0-8212-2022-5 (pb)
    1. Decoration and ornament,
    Rustic. 2. Interior decoration.
I. Title.
NK1986.R8T74   1991
747—dc20   90-55459

Bulfinch Press is an imprint and
trademark of Little, Brown and
Company (Inc.)

PRINTED IN SINGAPORE

CONTENTS

INTRODUCTION

Interior decoration, in the decade or so in which I have been involved with it in one way or another, seems to have got above itself somehow, to have become altogether too solemn an affair, all to do with spending money and showing off and drowning in chintz. Our first imperative when restoring the Old Chapel – our bolt-hole in Somerset – was to keep it a rudimentary sort of place, undemanding, unstructured, absolutely unsmart. On the other hand, we weren't going as far as minimalism. I enjoy minimalism, in photographs. In real life I like a degree of creature comfort, so the game has been to smuggle in comfortable seating, a stove, shelving and cupboards, favourite pictures, the sort of things that spell instant homeliness (comforting after a long drive late on a winter night) without cluttering up our big, simple space.

The Chapel is a weekend refuge, but I really did *live* in the country for eight years, on the edge of a small seaside town in Dorset. Those were the incredibly energetic days when I made my own pasta, rolled rough puff pastry, wove

lavender bottles to put between the sheets and was convinced I had discovered the secret of the good life, what the French more prettily call 'douceur de vivre'. I learned also to respect the seasons as they came, to bide my time during the numbing siege of a dark, grey, storm-lashed winter, putting my senses on hold for the duration, and to become a little delirious over the first patch of primroses, so fresh and composed in their buttery newness, on a steep bank in the late February sun.

My life during the past ten years could hardly have been more different. I now live most of the time in a Bengali village, improbably sited within five minutes' walk of London's deepest pinstripe City, with a night-time view from my top floor of the twinkling mast of the NatWest tower on the left, and the fierce obelisk of Hawksmoor's masterpiece, Christ Church, Spitalfields, prodding the sodium-lit nightscape to the right. The resident blackbird strikes up at dawn just minutes before the muezzin is relayed by loudspeaker from the gingerbread mosque in Whitechapel, and the air I step out into of a morning is redolent of fenugreek, from a hundred take-away samosa joints in and around Brick Lane.

After five years or so of buzzing to and fro, journalistically, domestically, in this most urban of environments, I knew with absolute, imperious finality that if I didn't have a bolt-hole in some green, inviolate, rural spot, I would whizz and twang myself to smithereens. A nasty bout of illness drove the point home. The Old Chapel, Laverton, a hamlet in a dip between low Mendip hills with the Westbury White Horse capering on a distant scarp, a few miles out of Bath, dropped into our lives at one of those critical moments, when it is tempting to see some pattern of destiny forming before one's eyes. I never believed I would find a house by going shopping for it. We did not even have to visit estate agents in the West Country. A friend of a friend heard the Chapel was up for sale, and told her friend, who loved it but couldn't see herself raising the money to restore – and partially re-build – what had once been a trim, compact, handsomely crafted Baptist chapel, of the local grey-blonde stone, built, as lead numerals on the facade proclaimed, in 1839, but in the style – as often happens in remoter country districts – fashionable a decade or two earlier. When Irma saw the chapel, it had been used for years as a barn by the farmer who owned the land. Elegant round-headed Georgian windows were smashed, light shafted through gaps in the roof tiles, the wooden floor had

rotted through, the one gravestone in the tiny adjacent churchyard leaned at an angle in a fuzz of nettles bisected by an unlovely cement path. There was no water or electricity, no sanitation, just a stone shell with a wooden gallery full of rotting pews, and a little vestry, which was also once a schoolhouse, tacked on to one side. But a rutted lane ran past, and beyond it a crinkly oak and a stolid pine, their feet in a hidden stream, and past that, a gentle curve of pasture land. Irma loved it so much she was almost tearful when she phoned me to say that if she couldn't bloody well have it, she wanted to make sure it went to people she liked and trusted. A feisty Brooklyner, she dreaded the clammy touch of improving estate agents, the thought of patios and a drive-in garage, of the soaring space which the Baptists had filled with singing being laterally divided to make a 'normal' house.

I did not, and I felt a churl for it, fall in love with the Chapel at first sight; on a grey day, dumped on the rim of a

ploughed field, it struck me as utilitarian, a stern little box of a place, and the poor solitary gravestone cast a chill. But within minutes I caught myself spinning plans – 'A tree over there, paving and herbs in the – um – churchyard, doors through at the back to let the countryside in . . .' and I knew down to my boots that this old, hidden-away, modest little piece of Somerset was offering me a haven, a place where the green fuse, to mess Dylan's metaphor around a little, could be well earthed.

I live with a modern architect and converting the chapel was the first joint building venture Richard and I had undertaken. I anticipated fierce argument and sure enough, we did argue, but less than might have been foretold and rarely about the crunchy decisions. We agreed for instance about the need to keep the chapel space intact. This means that we sleep on a bed cantilevered out on the gallery (page 10), which remains part of the main space. Less privacy, of course, but it is refreshing to dip into open plan living as a

change from living most of the time in a house with so many doors, and rooms, one never quite knows who is where. And waking on a sunny morning with a dress circle view out through the twelve-foot high arched windows on the opposite wall of the chapel (page 7) is perfection. Dutch Elm disease denuded our part of Somerset, according to our neighbour, Brian Rossiter, usually glimpsed briefly grinning from the high seat of his tractor, bumping off to tend his widely scattered acres. But as luck would have it a pair of bushy top trees remain on the skyline, neatly contained within the top segment of the window arches as I lazily survey the outside world from my pillow.

The first potential battle, over whether to punch doors out at ground level roughly each side of where the original Baptist altar might have stood, was somehow 'negotiated' without bloodshed. I was convinced that the existing traditional chapel fenestration, with light slanting in from windows high up on the wall, would give the feeling of living

at the bottom of a well, and we would feel frustratedly cut off from the countryside around. I suppose I imagined a couple of French windows carrying on the tall arched windows above to ground level, but Richard felt challenged to design something more vigorous, and as a result the chapel now has two elegant Vanbrugh-like doorways (page 7) opening to date onto a hollow filled with rubble and stone, one day to become a paved semi-circle with a curved stone seat dripping with shade-loving plants.

Where the resident architect really scored, however, was in contriving to pack three bedrooms, albeit small and oddly shaped, a tiny bathroom, and what in architectural parlance is called a vestibule, into a small though lofty former vestry, all without interfering with its spirited and elegant late Georgian fenestration. A less ingenious conver-

sion would have been forced to run a floor across the tall windows, which in Richard's solution remain the chief beauty of the austere little building, awash with light, framing the trees across the lane where birds in spring dart and swoop like busy shuttles. We have thoroughly secularized the main body of the chapel, what with the Vanbrugh doorways and an old Danish cast iron stove standing where the altar once presided, its twenty feet of stove pipe beaming out welcome heat along its length.

Unexpectedly, though, architectural sleight of hand has conjured an atmosphere of meditative peacefulness in the converted vestry, which we call the annexe for no explicable reason. The slip of a bedroom on the ground floor, barely containing a double bed and a chest of drawers, is the oddest room, with a ceiling that leaps from low and snug at the bed end to the full height of its majestic window at the other, but it has a rare peacefulness, forming as it does a sort of side chapel offering a simple, calming rural view, of 'our' (which it is not) tutelary oak tree.

Left to himself, Richard would have probably gone in for white walls and minimalist furnishings. I cannot abide white walls in England, especially not Brilliant White, which has the glare of false teeth in our soft climate. The working compromise is that I add colour, but low key. The decoration of the Chapel has happened in bursts of effort, sometimes happily inspired, sometimes less so, colours being, a sensitive, intuitive area that flows easily and harmoniously when ones personal energies are racing and eager, and lapses in times of discouragement. Although I am now trading in decorating kits, I did not have the Chapel in mind when I worked out our Colourwash formula, yet its combination of pure colour with rustic texture seemed exactly right for the limpid fresco look I felt these clear spaces needed. The sky, or cerulean, blue I have used in the little bedroom gives me the greatest satisfaction. The British tend to avoid blues, as cold colours, but this translucent, faintly greenish shade has a gentle gravity about it which has brought out the special atmosphere of a room which I hope is soothing to the family and friends who temporarily inhabit it.

My first decorative love was barge painting, then American folk art, and latterly, Scandinavian provincial decorative work, innocently daring in its use of colour and texture and *trompe l'oeil*. We haven't tried for folksiness in the Chapel, but somehow a certain hippyish flavour keeps creeping in, perhaps because rustic Indian textiles, colours and patterns settle remarkably easily into our own rustic, though quite different, context. But aside from the three piece suite, rattan, new and easy to live with, all the furnishing has been a job lot of hand-me-downs, white elephants, bits and pieces bought in flea markets which looked uneasy in our London home. It has become almost a point of honour not to spend (not that there was any cash left anyway after all the building costs had been taken care of) but to improvise. The game is to make all these disparate bits of junk knit together, visually and practically, and achieving this (we aren't quite there, but nearly) is a challenge which I particularly enjoy, giving non-serious scope for paint effects, or for a sudden brainwave which makes use at last of a bolt of fabric mouldering in a drawer. My best thought to date was to make use of the oddments of marble, some broken

washstand tops, some vaguely funeral fragments, which we inherited with the Chapel, to floor the diminutive bathroom in – for once in my life, as an exponent of *faux* finishes – real marble paving.

The delight of my decorating ventures in the Chapel, such as they are, is that they are private experiments, unpressurized, ultimately for my own instruction and pleasure, though I always hope other people will enjoy the results without realizing what it is they are enjoying. If they feel that life is somehow intensified, and this has something to do with the colours I have used inside the Chapel as well as the green hills around – well, that's compliment enough.

JOCASTA INNES

THE VIEW FROM WITHOUT

AUTUMN HOLLOW
This half-timbered cottage
(left) nestling in a hollow is
constructed of stone and
rendered brick. The steeply
pitched roof, the shutters, the
lavish window box displays and
the smoking chimney are typical
country features. Doorknockers,
like this clenched hand (above),
are often the object of
imaginative whimsy.

The style of the country is invariably one of simplicity and practicality, developed as a natural response to the landscape and the local conditions. The scale, the materials, the colours and the building techniques might be vastly different. But whether a tiny thatched-roof cottage, a weather-board villa with verandahs, or a large, rambling, stone country house, the approach is similar: an honest use of materials, a directness of purpose, and an ease with proportions. And there is always a sense of place and tradition, which manifests itself in the use of local materials – for instance, marble facings in central Italy near the quarries of Carrarra, or slate roofs in Wales – and in the types of ornamentation, such as interlaced wrought-iron work in Louisiana, pargetting (ornamental plasterwork) in eastern England, and decorative barge-boards on French and Dutch farmhouses.

The archetypal English country cottage inspired the architects of the Arts and Crafts Movement, which was formed in the mid-nineteenth century as a reaction to the 'manufactured' ethos of the Industrial Revolution; the aim was to rescue ancient skills and crafts from extinction. The Red House near London, designed for William Morris by Philip Webb in 1860, was a hymn to the traditional domestic buildings of the country. Webb and the other Arts and Crafts architects followed the general rules of the country builder, notably in the use of local materials and building techniques, but they stretched the vernacular vocabulary to create the wonderful sprawling villas exemplified by Henry Hobson Richardson's Watts Sherman House on Rhode Island, which is built of brick and stone with a pitched and gabled roof, and Greene and Greene's Gamble House in California, a house clad in shingles. Frank Lloyd Wright took the idea of using local materials and skills to the extreme when he built a series of Californian houses out of bricks made from sand found on site.

In the hands of the Arts and Crafts architects, the humble country cottage became Architecture. Many of the houses they built in the later nineteenth century were copied throughout the western world, providing the models for the country cottages of this century.

LOCAL DIVERSITY
The most successful country exteriors give the impression that they are an almost natural part of their surroundings. A beautiful old English cottage (left) with slate roof is festooned with climbing roses. The fine arched doorway frames the entrance to a dark hall and mysteries beyond.

In contrast, much of the charm of this early eighteenth-century cottage in Connecticut (top right) lies in its simple detailing and clear lines. Painted a very pale yellow with white facings and a green door, the weather-board cottage is designed around a central fireplace, positioned where it will warm the whole house.

Dark Finnish-style weather-board (bottom right) melts into a pine forest. The timber is stained a dark brown with the window and roof facings left unstained for decorative effect. The planks of wood have been slotted together at the corners so that the structure expands and contracts naturally with the extremes of temperature, thus avoiding the conflict that occurs between wood and metal.

A row of almshouses in Essex (overleaf) has the distinctive pink-tinted plaster walls traditional in the region, barge-boarding, and tiled roofs. On the left is a row of older houses with thatched roofs.

FRENCH SUPPORT
In the porch of this French cottage (left) a heavy structural beam is supported on a thick squared timber column which, in turn, is strengthened with diagonal beams. A similar structure can be erected to disguise an ugly house wall or too large windows, making a perfect support for tendrils of wisteria, as here.

FRAGRANT BEAUTY
Climbing plants are an obvious way of enlivening an uninteresting exterior, particularly clematis, which wreaths this house (right). Several of the clematis species are evergreens, providing cover throughout the year as well as blooms in spring and summer. To provide a long flowering season, plant different types.

LEAFY PLEASURES
Pelargonium flowers (left), which will last all summer long, spill out of a trio of similarly shaped pots beside a half-barrel full of great leafy foliage.

An espaliered tree (below) has been trained to frame a window, an ingenious and decorative method of softening a plain feature.

CLIMBING DECORATION

Decide which of the two main types of climber is most suited to your property before planting.
- Self-clingers such as *Hydrangea petiolaris*, Virginia creeper and ivy. These require little training and care, but if the wall is old and crumbling they can cause damage, and if wall maintenance is required the plant may be ruined when pulled off.
- Climbers requiring support such as clematis, roses and summer jasmine. These need supporting trellis or wires and careful training, but they can easily be taken down.

MATERIALS

Wood is often the cheapest and most easily accessible material. It provides the framework for buildings throughout the world, and has been widely used in the wooden bungalow that is found throughout North America, Australia and New Zealand. Like the stone farmhouses of Europe, the bungalows are similar in basic style, but they differ according to local conditions. For instance, the verandahs of the New Zealand version are generally narrower than those in Australia, which has a hotter climate; there the verandahs are used as outdoor rooms – as dining areas or living rooms. The type of ornamentation – the cast-iron or wooden decorative work – varies from area to area, according to the patterns produced by local firms or craftsmen.

In country cottages throughout Europe stone is the prevalent material. Small two-storey Irish cottages are made of field stones picked from the ground. The yellowish limestone of the English Cotswolds and the red and ochre stones of Roussillon in the south of France, like the sandstone often used in Texas ranch houses, are quarried in the region and cut into large blocks. The types of roofing reflect the regional character too: in the Cotswolds slate is used, rounded red tiles are characteristic of the Mediterranean area, and the Texas stone and mortar house is roofed with wooden shingles. In some regions the stone walls are covered with stucco or colourful mixtures of local earth and sand.

Earth is moulded into low-storey houses with flat roofs, called adobes, in Mexico and the south-western United States. It is a technique long used by the Native Americans and adopted by the Spanish colonists, who mixed the earth and sand with straw and shaped it into bricks which were dried in the sun, a method they learnt in North Africa.

Fired bricks in the familiar rectangular shape are used all over Europe and parts of the New World. European settlers, most notably the Dutch, imported bricks and brick-making techniques into America. They also brought their shaped gables and patterned brickwork: red and grey bricks would be laid in a diaper (diamond) pattern, for example, or in a Flemish bond, in which risers (the short end) and stretchers (the long side) are alternated.

GABLE ENDS
The slates covering this steeply pitched roof (above) well illustrate the tonal differences found in natural materials.

LINEAR COMPOSITION
Timber walls (right) made of broad vertical planks have weathered into many gradations of colour.

FRENCH THATCH
Traditional white plastered
walls (above) act as the support
for a well-constructed thatched
roof in this French cottage.

IRON AND PLASTER

The details of an exterior count towards the total effect. This iron door handle and knocker (above left) are a wonderful example of the great skill and instinctive understanding of materials found in much traditional craftwork.

Daub and wattle walls (above right) contrast white plaster with beams turned a silvery grey by age.

BRICK AND WOOD
A herringbone pattern of very long, narrow burnt-orange bricks
(above left) has been laid in a thin concrete bordered by thick beams
coloured ochre.
    A simple, weathered-wood door (above right) made of roughly
cut planks, is strengthened with a cross beam and furnished with
utilitarian iron bolts and door latch.

TEXTURES AND COLOURS

SHUTTERS WITHOUT

Crisp white window frames in a French house (above) are bordered by natural stone facings against rust-coloured render. The bright blue used for the simple wooden shutters is a particularly strong contrast to the rust: the two colours are natural opposites.

COLOUR WITHIN

The weather-board wall of this eighteenth-century Connecticut house (right) is made of thin overlapping boards laid horizontally and painted a traditional strong farmhouse red. Colour contrast comes in this instance from the interior shutters.

The textural play of material against material – brick and mortar, rough-cut and highly polished stones, rendered walls and painted woodwork – is a great part of the attraction of the country cottage.

One material may be used for the walls, another for facing the windows and doors; a third for the roof, and yet another for decorative effects: painted rough-cast walls with faceted corner-stones, plaster around the painted windows and doors, and a slate roof on a typical English cottage, for example, or uneven pieces of stone fixed with a smooth-grained mortar with wooden window and door frames and a tiled roof in Italy. Or the same material is cut in varied shapes, laid in opposite directions or finished in a different manner. Horizontal wooden cladding is an obvious example, used with a shingled roof and decorative barge-boards. In an adobe, the openings for doors and windows are often highlighted by rounded indentations in the wall surface or simply by a thick band of colour.

Everything else about a house may be perfect, but if it is painted a colour that is out of keeping with the neighbourhood it will look wrong. When choosing a new scheme for your house, look at the colours around you, and research the traditions of the region. The cinnabars, ochres, verdet greens, and rose madders of the French, Irish and English countrysides give way to clearer colours close to the Mediterranean. In North America, the palette ranges from white through red to black. Combining hot with strong – red and yellow, red and bright pink, a blue-violet with emerald green – is a favourite device of the Mexicans. The Greeks and the Scandinavians use the reflective qualities of white to emphasize the blueness of sea and sky.

The easiest way to make an exterior more interesting and more in keeping with the country style is with texture and colour. Stripping inappropriate gloss paint or an unsympathetic colour off the woodwork and replacing it with something more in harmony with the wall colour is an inexpensive improvement. Trellises can be added to frame a doorway or window or simply to add interest to a wall; painting it a different colour from the wall draws attention to the trellis, and growing plants over it introduces new dimensions of colour and texture. A bungalow made of uniform harshly coloured bricks can be painted white or disguised with ivy or other climbing plants, large picture windows can be disguised by a pergola or porch, and entrances softened with plants or tall ceramic pots. A more costly option is to stucco walls then paint or wash them.

BAMBOO SHOOTS
Short pieces of bamboo strung together make a curtain (above) that provides an unusual screen for a door as blue as the Ibiza sky overhead and doubles as soothing wind chimes.

COUNTRY HUES
The stronger light of the country invites the use of clear tones that would look out of place against the comparative monochrome of the city: a raspberry-coloured shutter (top right) contrasts with custard-yellow plaster walls; the luminous sea green used on a door (top far right) richly complements the clear yellow-green vine leaves; an acid-yellow wall (right) provides a lovely backdrop to a terracotta urn.

WINDOWS AND DOORS

The patterns made by windows and doors add the real character to a building. How they are placed, their shape and their size influence the look of the whole elevation, and are traditionally based on the rules of proportion. These simple rules are universal, instinctively understood by the Shaker and the Mexican, the Australian colonist and the English village builder alike: they order the relationship of doors to windows, and of ground-floor windows to those on the floors above, as well as of the size and shape of the roof to the flat planes of the walls of the building, and the appropriateness of ornamentation.

If the windows are too wide or too large, their shape can be altered by the addition of half-open shutters, by planting, or by painting the glazing bars black. The window openings of narrow or small windows can be painted white, and the addition of open shutters will have the effect of making them appear wider. Aluminium window frames are never appropriate in country-style homes.

From the street, the house may be hidden behind high evergreen hedges, brick walls or painted picket fences. The view from the gateway or the street to the house draws the eye to the front door, the focal point of the country exterior. If the door is out of character with the architecture, it will destroy the whole look of the house; the best approach is often to replace the door with one that is more sympathetic and to soften the entrance way with climbing plants and sprawling lavender bushes. The colour is as important as the style of the door in creating the right impression. It should be in keeping with the texture of the surrounding walls and the local light: in colder countries bold simple colours – dark green, black or red – are favoured, while soft blues and greens, pinks and yellows work well in sunnier climes. The country style does not depend on historical detailing for its success but has a more eclectic and instinctive feel. Odd decorative objects from any period or style – terracotta panels, marble columns, wooden finials, a rooster weather-vane – will add a distinctive charm to the entrance way.

OPEN AND SHUT

Dressing a door or window can be a simple way of introducing the country look to an exterior.

Plaster casts (far left) sit in the sun on a tiled window sill. The pale grey wooden shutters with diamond cut-outs are subtly shaded in keeping with the mud and stone wall.

A beautifully simple inner door (left), white with deep windows, has a lace shawl draped behind it – the softness of the effect contrasting with the strength of the bold blue outer door. The gently arched doorway is outlined by a cream band.

SCHOOLHOUSE SIMPLICITY

The white weather-board walls and plain green shutters, shingled roof and white picket fence and gate of this New England schoolhouse are typical of the traditional buildings of this part of North America. All the elements unite in an elegant, unfussy functionality that represents the best of country style exteriors.

HALLS AND STAIRWAYS

UNDERSTATED DRAMA
The original worn flagstones
and beamed ceiling in this
entrance hall (left) are
combined with knotted
architraves plaster walls, and
country cupboards. A good-sized
entrance hall, like this one, can
double as a dining hall.
   Basketware and wooden
butter moulds (above) are good
examples of the natural beauty
of everyday objects created by
country artisans.

The intrinsic welcome of natural materials and the comfortable look of uncontrived interiors seen through the doorway of a country house are characteristic of the style. In some country homes you can stand at the front door and see right down the hallway to the back garden, with the light that escapes from adjoining rooms casting playful shadows. In others, the entrance hall is shut off by doors or by thick curtains, and what is behind them is revealed gradually – and selectively.

The character of halls and stairways is affected by the colours, textures and patterns continually glimpsed through open doorways. They may be quite small spaces, especially in modern apartments, so you can afford to be extravagant: a front hallway of marblized walls with a slate floor, for instance, oak parquet from front entrance to back door, or William Morris wallpapers and Oriental-patterned carpet runners through every passageway and up every stair.

NORWEGIAN WOOD

A variety of wood and paint tones and textures gives a special warmth to this hallway. The effect is emphasized by the rag rugs and wall-hanging, an old chest brimming with chopped wood, a painted bureau and a pair of beautiful, worn, side chairs.

CAMOUFLAGE

Pale grey walls conceal cupboard doors that have been painted the same colour as the wall – a favourite country device. Instead of using a large piece of free-standing furniture, one of the cupboards has been built into a corner, making an interesting angled wall.

ENTRANCE HALLS

AGED PANELS
The elegance of the wooden panelling darkened by age in this cottage (left) is all the more impressive when you look closely and notice its simple construction. The small pedestal table and nineteenth-century cane-seated chair complement the wood.

SECURE DOOR
Heavy iron hinges and bolts signal the strength of this hinged door (above), and a solidity belied by its soft green colour and the delicate leadlight above. Beautiful greyish-green and cream tiles and a French, painted chair with floral cushions introduce subtle pattern.

The entrance hall in a country-style home is a half-way area between the outdoors and the warmth and shelter of indoors. Here, the floors are notable for their good looks as well as their practical qualities: wood in planks or parquet, worn flagstones, warm-toned quarry tiles, reddish brick or black-and-white tiles, and more often than not some sort of rug or mat to add textural interest. The walls are painted, papered or lined, and may be treated more extravagantly than those of other passageways: the entrance hall could be delineated by *trompe-l'oeil* stonework, a dado of encaustic tiles, or lined with beautiful wood panelling. Traditionally there is somewhere to hang overcoats and leave umbrellas and, usually, a table for letters and papers, which could be ornamented with a blue-and-white bowl full of deep red pot pourri or a spherical glass vase of pink roses.

The ideal entrance hall, as found in grander country homes, is a large roomy space, with hallways leading off into the private areas of the house and a prominent stairway to the upper floors. In a wood-panelled, stone-floored medieval-style hall the main pieces of furniture might be a settle – a wooden three- or four-person seat with a panelled back and baluster legs – and a long oak table or an antique sideboard. The Italians place a solid but elegant stone garden bench against pale pinkish-ochre walls. An American-style entrance features white walls, checkered floor, antique tables, chests or cabinets and paintings of country scenes.

In many country cottages a second door keeps out the cold and shuts off the entrance hall from the rest of the house. Usually glass-panelled and often incorporating stained or coloured glass, the door is set into a frame of interior windows. This is a good treatment for an entrance that continues straight up a narrow hallway. The device of a decorative arch is a good way to break up a long hall; hung with thick curtains, it marks the boundary between the public rooms traditionally located at the front of the house, and the bedrooms and kitchen at the back.

Allow for storage of coats, umbrellas and winter boots in the entrance hall. If space allows, these items could be kept in a beautiful piece of furniture, such as a great bow-fronted cupboard, a particularly fine armoire, or an antique painted corner cabinet. Built-in walls or cupboards and drawers in Shaker style can be made in fine-textured or painted wood. This is a good solution in minute entrance halls where there is little extra space. In such a small area, painting the cupboards the same colour as the walls will have the effect of unifying the space, and white or a pale shade will make it appear larger.

Many apartments have a small entrance hall only, with no other passageways or staircases. In this situation the use of locally made quarry tiles, bricks laid in a herringbone pattern or hand-cut, pegged oak boards on the floor will immediately indicate the country style, and walls and doors can be given a simple, uncluttered treatment.

The look of the inner side of the front door is, to a certain extent, dictated by security considerations. The solid steel door favoured by many urban apartment dwellers can be disguised by a more rustic inner door, or by a decorative panel. But it will never be a totally successful substitute for the classic plank, glazed or panelled door.

MUDROOMS

A shelf-cum-coat rack placed high on a back hall wall (far left) makes good use of space as well as providing storage for odds and ends that are difficult to place. Shopping baskets are hung from hooks in the ceiling.

A roomy back entrance hall (left) doubles as a spare bedroom. Clothes and logs create a still life beside an unusual 'brick-framed' fireplace which appears suspended.

There is no reason why ordinary objects such as rubber boots (above) should be hidden away. Here, they have pride of place along with an antique tennis racquet, an old oar and a fishing net.

MAKING THE MOST OF HALL SPACE

In country cottages it is usual to take advantage of every spare bit of space; halls and stairways are valuable sources.

- Support painted or varnished wooden shelves with battens or curved wooden or iron brackets. If you have to use metal strip brackets, paint them to match the wall.
- Use rows of narrow shelves or shelving units to store books in a passage; wicker baskets on wider shelves can be used instead of drawers; slatted shelves can be used for storing country produce and preserves.
- Hang outdoor clothes, dog leads and sports equipment from brass hooks fixed below shelves, traditional coat and hat racks (more space-saving than a coat stand) or a Shaker-style peg rail.
- Fix large hooks to ceiling beams to store shopping baskets or dried flowers. Use butchers' hooks to hang things from an old-fashioned wooden laundry rack which can be suspended from a high ceiling or stairwell.

HALLS, PASSAGES AND LANDINGS

EARTHY TONES
The grand scale of a classically shaped pottery pitcher (above) set on a built-in shelf dominates this colour-washed stairwell with its rough vertical beams. Its strong form is in contrast to the collection of little glass bottles and wooden clogs set on the window ledge at the turn of the stairs.

Because hallways and landings are subjected to heavy use, surfaces and finishes need to be chosen for their durability as well as looks. In country interiors the emphasis is on natural materials, and much is made of the floor, which is the most telling decorative element in these transitional spaces.

Floors in the hallways and landings can be used to define spaces. The boundaries delineating public areas from private ones are often marked by showy materials, such as marble or encaustic tiles, in the front part of the house, with less expensive woods, linoleum or carpet used in the areas that are not on view. Or the hall floor may be well-worn marble studded with small dark diamonds, leading to rooms with wooden floors covered in Oriental-patterned carpets – an effective way to contrast colour, texture and feel. Another approach is to use the same flooring throughout the halls and rooms, thus providing a feeling of continuity: polished floorboards, for instance, or, as in many old farmhouses, a ground-level floor of flagstones.

Treating the lower section of the wall, the dado, differently from the upper part is a traditional and practical feature of the country hallway. If hard-wearing tongue-and-groove panelling and heavy embossed wallpapers are painted in a stronger version of the colour used on the plain upper walls, the passageway is made to appear wider than it really is and the change of surfaces is emphasized. However, even if the entire wall is decorated in the same colour, interest is created by the contrast of textures. Mixing different wallpaper designs – small florals with larger ones, for instance – is a device favoured by the Victorians. A dado can also be 'faked': a stronger colour used on the lower part of plaster walls, a wallpaper or stencilled border placed at dado-rail height, or a faux stone dado, painted on.

If the hallway is too high – which is often the case in apartments that have been converted from large private houses – you can make it seem lower by continuing the ceiling colour down to picture-rail height. A dark ceiling colour will emphasize the effect; with a white or very pale ceiling it will not be so pronounced.

Odd-shaped ceilings, walls and architectural features are common in country cottages, and they are often treated with panache: the slope of a ceiling can be followed with a stencilled frieze, an uneven window or door frame can be outlined in a hand-painted stripe, a round window framed in a carved wooden square.

WEAVE AND QUILT
The emphasis is on the delicate tracery of table baskets in this landing display (above). Below it a collection of softly faded quilted bedcovers has been casually stacked on a chair, with characteristically country nonchalance.

Doors and door frames are best treated simply. Wood that has been stripped or polished, and paint that is the same, or similar, colour as the walls or the dado are often the best choices. Solid panelled doors can be glazed, allowing natural light into the hall; plain doors are good backgrounds for *trompe-l'oeil* panels or stencilled decoration.

Landings often have dead spaces, ideal for displaying a special collection or providing much needed storage. Narrow triangular cupboards can be fitted in on the turn of the stairs, blanket boxes can double as seats on small square landings, long thin sideboards or serving tables provide handsome showcases for a clutter of different-shaped vases, all crammed with fresh flowers, leaves and grasses.

COUNTRY TIDY
A capacious armoire (above) fits snugly under the low-beamed ceiling in an out-of-the-way corner created when a door was bricked up. The beams have been painted cream like the walls, which has a lighter effect than if they had been left unpainted.

STAIRCASES

TROMPE-L'OEIL
The detailed geometric design
painted on this staircase (right)
is a very effective alternative to
a stair carpet. The density of
pattern necessitates a simple
approach to the surroundings –
in this case plain white paint –
if the overall result is not to
overwhelm.

CLASSIC LINES
Grey has been used on the
skirting boards and to follow
the gradient of the steps,
making a subtle diagonal
(right). This simple decorative
device emphasizes the clean
lines and perfect finish of what
is a straightforward wooden
staircase.

A staircase is the architectural showpiece of the country-style house. Styles are varied, the most common being between one and one-and-a-half metres (3-5 ft) wide, cased in or with straight balusters and a fairly plain newel post. Variations of this theme include turned and hand-carved balusters and newel posts, grooved handrails, and carved and painted panels. Centrally-positioned staircases branching into matching sets of steps are more dramatic than the stairs that hug the walls of a compact stairwell. At the opposite extreme is the rudimentary ladder leading to attic rooms.

The standard wooden stairs found in the Australian villa, the New England weatherboard house, and the nineteenth-century English cottage are usually left polished or painted, and sometimes carpeted with a bordered runner – firmly attached for safety – which emphasizes the rippling lines of the stairs and the natural play of light and dark created by treads and risers. The Shakers stencilled patterns on the

risers, leaving the treads and banisters in unpolished wood. In adobes or Italian farmhouses, the stairs are made of hard materials such as concrete or stone – cold and solid. The Italians leave the stone unadorned, while in the adobes the stairs are painted like all the walls and ceilings, sometimes in very bright colours.

Dados are occasionally sloped up the side of the stairs, but usually are continued only along the dado-rail level. The stair gradient may be followed by skirting or similar linear decoration. Sometimes these lines are joined to horizontals marking the upper-floor level; this creates an interesting area that can be decorated with a mural or stencils.

The stairwell, generally the highest uninterrupted wall in the house, can be turned into a picture gallery of full-length portraits or pastoral scenes, or used to show off collections of walking sticks or antique bridles. Straw hats, boots, woven bags and umbrellas are conveniently at hand when hung from lines slung between balusters.

CONTRASTING ASCENTS
The architectural qualities of this wonderful stone staircase (left) need no embellishment. The stairs, made of unmatched stone blocks, flare out at the bottom, creating a natural place to sit in the generous-sized hallway.

In contrast, the focus of this coir-covered staircase (above) is an ornately carved balustrade which doubles back sharply to create an elaborate linear pattern. The space by stairs is often wasted; here it is piled with unusual rustic baskets.

BOLD BEAUTY

A modern approach in a
Mexican house (right) is to
build an enclosed staircase out
of what appear to be structural
beams. Everything about this
simple staircase is consistent
with the way the rest of the
interior has been treated –
pink, rough-textured walls and
solid floor and woodwork – and
much is made of the sunlight
that casts wavy shadows through
the slatted ceiling.

FRENCH STYLE

Two unmatched staircases (far
right) have been built to
measure in the upper storeys of
this old French country cottage.
Just as a room is somehow fitted
under the eaves whenever more
space is needed, so an extra step
is added on what appears to be
an ad hoc basis. The treads are
covered in worn terracotta tiles
edged with wood and the risers
are plastered to match the walls.

RISING STEPS

The risers of a staircase, which are not subject to heavy wear, can be decorated. The simplest approach is to follow the Shakers and combine scrubbed wooden treads with risers that are painted white or cream. These can be left bare, but they look very effective if stencilled or hand-painted.

● A simple centred design, such as a bird or motif, can be repeated on every step.

● Paint every step with a different but related image such as a series of flowers, toys, or animals.

● Cover the risers with an all-over pattern – two-colour geometrics or an Italianate design work well.

As alternatives to paintings, flat metal cut-outs of traditional images, such as weather-vanes, houses, stars or hearts can be attached to risers, or they can be covered with beautiful patterned tiles that are too fragile to use on floors.

LIVING ROOMS

ESSENTIAL COUNTRY
The assured mix of colours,
patterns and textures in this
living room (left) is the true
essence of the country style. The
floor-to-ceiling stack of logs at
the side of the fireplace is a
witty, but also utilitarian
addition. A curved iron keyhole
(above) is an eye-catching detail
in a painted door.

Relaxing comfortably in a well-sprung chintz-covered armchair by a roaring fire with flames flickering over the walls, the dog curled up in front of the hearth, books piled casually over side tables and floor, and the fragrance of garden blooms mingling with the scented smoke from burning logs, you could be forgiven for thinking you are in a pastoral paradise.

The country-style living room is all about comfort and conviviality. The attraction of natural materials, hand-crafted furniture and objects, regional styles, cherished possessions, and patterns and colours inspired by the countryside lies in the winning combination of the traditional, the personal and the eclectic. It works equally well in an urban environment as it does in the country and, because it does not rely on a slavish devotion to style or to architecture, it can be adapted to suit any home, whatever its age or condition.

A common approach is to use white or a very pale colour all over the walls, regardless of whether there is any change of surface, as with a dado or picture rail. Sometimes these architectural features are emphasized, by the use of a patterned wallpaper, for instance, or a change of colour. Alternatively, effects may be faked: a dado could be painted to look like slabs of stone, or a cornice replaced with a stencilled border or a thick stripe of colour.

Deeper colours can look very heavy and dull, so a good solution is to 'break up' the colour by applying it over a lighter or contrasting background colour – as you do when using such techniques as colour-washing, rag-rolling or sponging. This has the effect of adding a sense of life and movement to the wall and such paint effects against plain paint are common in country-style rooms.

For floors, painted boards, oak parquet waxed and worn to a mellow patina, monumental stone slabs, a herringbone pattern of glazed bricks and traditional warm-toned quarry tiles all possess a timeless beauty, and create a solid foundation for a country living room. If the material of the floor is less intrinsically interesting it can be painted in rug and tile designs, combed in bold contrasting colours, or stencilled with delicate sprays of flowers. Wall-to-wall carpet looks best if broken up by rugs: hooked folk-art rugs with abstract or pictorial designs, colourful rag rugs made of scraps of old fabric, Oriental-style patterns and coir matting are all found in the country living room. A large rug may cover the entire floor; smaller ones can be placed in front of the fireplace or in a circle made by chairs.

PRACTICAL COMFORT
This room (left), which serves
many purposes, is the most
heavily used in the house, where
the owners can relax and
entertain, watch television or
work. Being a room that is both
in everyday use and a suitable
place for entertaining, it is
versatile, with surfaces, fabrics
and furniture suitable for day
and evening, family and more
formal occasions.

COLOUR SCHEMES
The muted pinks and oranges
in this colourful living room
(above) have been combined
with a variety of textures —
rough plaster, beams, polished
mahogany, woven kelims,
cottons and crocheted blanket.
The danger of blandness in
a white-on-white room
(overleaf) has been averted with
the inclusion of striking pieces
of dark furniture and folk art.

COLOUR, TEXTURE
AND PATTERN

OLD AGE
There has been no attempt to
disguise the age of these shutters
(above) in an eighteenth-
century Connecticut house.
They are painted a traditional
blue-grey, and the colour is
repeated in the hand-blocked
wallpaper.

The centrepiece in this
French living room (right) is
the blue-and-orange painted
ceiling, in which naïve birds
and leaves are intermingled
with more formal Florentine
motifs. The room has the
uncontrived elegance that relies
on texture rather than colour
for its visual interest.

The colours of the spectrum can be divided into those that are 'warm' – reds, oranges, yellows – and 'cool' ones – blues, greens and violets. Only in the hottest climates are the strongest versions of these colours widely used. Elsewhere, interiors are in subtle and muted shades such as pinks, pale greens, soft yellows, powder blue, ochre. But even here there is an important place for vivid and intense colours: bright red and sky blue patches in a quilt, for instance, or an emerald green dado.

The stone slab or the pale yellow painted wall, however, is never a single 'flat' colour, but is uneven. Its colour varies because the texture of the material and the way light falls on its surface affect the density of the colour. Much of the appeal of the country interior comes from the inherent textural beauty of the natural materials used, and the play of texture against contrasting texture: a painted brick wall against window frames painted in a matt finish, the checkered effect of a tiled floor next to a coarsely woven linen chair cover, a pressed tin ceiling surrounded by a decorative plaster cornice.

Another dimension is added with pattern. The Victorians understood instinctively how to layer pattern upon pattern. They would mix the scale of the designs, combine the geometric with folk motifs, and frame the walls and floor with wonderful borders, unifying the scheme with one or two common colours. The wallpaper design might change at dado- or picture-rail height, and another pattern would be used on the ceiling. Highly decorative rugs were laid on top of patterned floor cloths or black-and-white tiles.

A similar innate assurance is much in evidence in the country interior, where the room appears to come together in a slightly haphazard way, rather than be contrived by a designer. Walls are painted in a favourite blue, an heirloom Oriental rug of deep reds and blues is thrown across the floor, a Bentwood chair rescued from the attic is placed next to a mahogany table found in a second-hand shop, and a patchwork quilt camouflages a plain calico sofa cover; indigo batik curtains might appear to add confusion but because their dominant colour is one that is found in the floor rug and quilt the room will work well.

BLUE MOODS
Blue is a favourite country colour, used, as here (left), with enough white and cream to lighten the effect. It provides a cool background for vivid accent colours: bright reds in the kelims, the glazed orange jug and Chinese red bowl. Strong geometric patterns in the kelim underpin the scheme.

FIREPLACES

The hypnotic quality of a warm fire draws people in to form a cosy circle. The undisputed focal point of the living room when the fire is lit, the fireplace is, in any case, the most important architectural feature of most rooms.

In early American cottages, fireplaces were built of brick with the mantel incorporated into the panelled wall; they were often large and designed to accommodate big cooking pots. On a similar scale are the handsome stone fireplaces of European farmhouses. More rudimentary are the openings supported by a great wooden beam found in some old English cottages, and the plain wooden mantelpieces – which are sometimes decorated with stencils or hand painted – common to country cottages. Smaller arched openings are characteristic of adobes; these sculptural niches are located as often in corners as in a central position in a room.

The French make great decorative use of bricks, laying them in a herringbone pattern in the inner fireplace, and then adding a stone or marble mantelpiece. Logs are placed

LACE MANTEL

A handmade lace border edges a mantel shelf (far left) full of china and enamelware. Pretty Victorian jugs are hung on hooks and autumnal-coloured dried flowers are hung from an old-fashioned clothes drier.

FIRE BRIGHT

The dominant feature of this living room (left) is the great fireplace. The high, leather-covered brass fireguard is a good place to sit and warm toes as well as providing protection for small children.

on andirons (also called dog-fires), which are pairs of iron L-shaped stands, or fire baskets are used. Sometimes, however, the bricks are lined with a decorative cast-iron plate with an integral grate; some have a border of tiles. In large-scale fireplaces hearths are usually made of stone or brick and are often raised above the level of the floor. In smaller and more elegant fireplaces marble, slate or tiles may be used.

A beautiful fireplace can transform a featureless room. It needs to be installed by a professional and the chimney must be checked thoroughly for cracks and fireproofing. If the room does not have a working chimney, use the fireplace simply as an architectural focus, as you do whenever a fire is not lit. Lay logs in brass-ended andirons; fill the grate with pine cones, dried flowers or wooden fruit and vegetables; or place a tapestry or hand-painted fire screen in front of the empty grate. Examples of folk art, such as weather vanes or painted wooden animals, can be used as screens too, and drift-wood and odd-shaped stones can be set on the hearth like pieces of sculpture.

The mantel shelf in country homes is used to display clocks, sculptures, groups of candlesticks, lamps, paintings, family photos, miniature rocking chairs, curios and blue-and-white ginger jars; bunches of flowers hang upside down drying; long rows of tiny red peppers are strung along the edge of the shelf.

Without question, there is a romance about a real fire, but making it – and cleaning up afterwards – can be a chore. Fortunately, the new generation of gas 'fake' fires not only look authentic and produce real flames but they can heat an average-sized room. Also in the practical vein are the traditional solid-fuel stoves which the Scandinavians favour rather than an open fire. They are more efficient heaters and can be linked to boilers to provide hot water and central heating. The enamelled stoves are generally white, often enchantingly decorated, and are set into a corner or out from a wall of the living room.

FURNITURE

SITTING PRETTY
An eighteenth-century Windsor rocker (left) is a traditional country chair, with a curved high back and arms.

Crisp cane is never out of place in a country-style room. Here (bottom left), it has been painted white and supplied with comfortable soft cushions.

Throwing a beautiful bed cover or blanket over a sofa (right) – here, a heavy white-on-white embroidered bedspread – is a favourite way of disguising shabby upholstery, creating a more informal atmosphere or ringing the seasonal changes.

White slipcovers (far right), attached with ties, are a casual and practical approach – covers can be easily made in strong cottons, heavy linens, ticking or glazed chintz.

T he most important pieces of furniture in a country living room are sofas and chairs. This is a room designed for recreation, and there must be something you can sink into and immediately feel relaxed.

Old-fashioned, amply proportioned sofas and armchairs that are well-sprung and have generous down-filled cushions are hard to beat, although they may look overbearing if the room is small. In that case, choose elegant two-seaters or sleeker modern versions but make sure they are well-endowed with comfortable cushions. The height of the arms is an important factor if you spend a lot of time reading: test that they are the right height to rest a book on before buying. The depth and height of the seats are worth checking too; your feet should be able to rest easily on the floor when you sit right back in the chair or sofa.

Outdoor wicker furniture, rocking chairs that include Bentwoods, ladderbacks, and Bostons, Lloyd Loom sofas and chairs, twig furniture, cane-sided suites, chunky

bamboo furniture, wing and club chairs, all sorts of polished and painted uprights and modern leather sofas look at home in the country living room, alongside built-in wooden settles and banquettes, and good-looking tapestry-covered stools and ottomans.

The alcoves on each side of a fireplace are the traditional place for shelving to keep books, magazines, records and stereos. A combination of a lower, closed cabinet with shelves above – either left open or with glazed doors – provides child-proof storage; freestanding bookcases in mellow woods or thick wooden shelves built into the walls are good-looking alternatives. If you have an extensive library, a wall of bookshelves can reach to the ceiling and be continued over doorways.

But you don't need to confine yourself to 'conventional' living-room furniture. Beautiful dish dressers can be used to display paintings and curios; an open blanket cabinet can show off a priceless collection of antique patchwork quilts, the top of an old farmhouse cupboard can be piled with wooden bowls or regional pottery.

Other pieces in the living room might include round pedestal tables and a low coffee table conveniently placed near chairs and sofas; a chest of drawers that is too big or too beautiful for the bedroom; and perhaps a piano. Even such 'modern' items as a small computer kept in a rolltop desk or an Alvar Aalto trolley for cocktails will only add to the eclectic atmosphere that is so much of the essence of the country style.

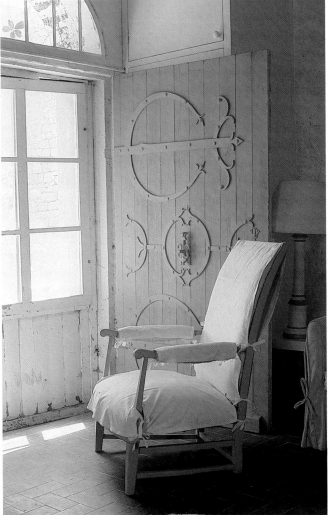

PAINT PERFECT
Painted furniture, whether antique or newly decorated, is one of the keynotes of the country style. A small French chair (left) which would be charming anyway with turned legs, curved back bars and rattan seat is even more appealing painted in blue and white. A large armoire (above), which would tend to dominate, has been softened with greeny turquoise pigment rubbed into a white undercoat. It now matches the floor, unifying the whole room.

FOLK-ART COLOUR
The blue-grey of this cabinet (left) is a timeless colour finish for furniture, inspired by the celadons of Chinese porcelain. Here, the paintwork has been left in its beautiful worn state.

A chest (below) with panels painted with stylized flowers has a rich, dark blue background. It is perfectly set off by the plank floor painted in black-and-yellow checks. The folk-art style is picked up in the collection of American baskets, the naïve painting and the candle holder.

FABRICS
AND FURNISHINGS

SIMPLE SHADES
Large and small patterns in different shades of blue have been mixed to great effect (above): a check slipover tied with bows for the chair, a tiny-patterned top cloth on the table, sprigged wallpaper and pretty lampshade and curtains with an ikat pattern.

SUN SHADES
Pinky-orange stripes and checks add extra warmth to this summery living room (right). The window-seat is stuffed with cushions and the floor has been covered with coir matting – hard wearing for a room with a lot of use but warm in tone – creating a welcoming effect.

The fabrics of the country are made of natural materials – cotton, linen, wool and silk. They are smooth- or rough-textured: thick velvets and ribbed needlecords, simple ticking and calicos, plain or printed glazed chintz and linens, rough-weaved wools and fine muslins, crewelwork embroideries and hard-wearing damasks. Patterns are printed or woven, and sometimes hand-painted: stripes, large brash florals, little sprigged leaves, batiks and paisleys, ginghams, warm-hued Provençal designs and splatter-dyed.

The typical chintz, plain calicos, ticking and delicate regional prints are used to cover furniture. Loose covers and plain tailored upholstery are popular, although one or two pieces which have been elaborately upholstered with tassels, braids and rich silks can be slipped in to offset the simplicity. A plain sofa can be enlivened by draping it with a Navajo Indian blanket, a Spanish shawl or a multicoloured patchwork quilt.

Cushions can be covered in the same fabric as the furniture, or in contrasting colours and patterns; whichever approach is taken, piles of unmatched cushions always add comfort and visual interest, particularly those made from kelims or tapestries. Shapes can vary from flat squares, through big envelopes and gusseted squares, to circles and rectangles and may be edged in braid, pleated into corners or left plain.

Generous curtains that sweep the floor are designed to keep in the warmth. Thick wools, rough linens and tough cottons, often fully lined, hang in soft pleats or gathered from brass rings and are sometimes combined with sheer curtains of muslin or lace. If you want a sculptural effect, use heavy canvas. Light, fine fabrics are often left unlined and trailing over the floor; they can be casually knotted, simply draped over the curtain rail, or held back with elaborately decorated sashes. Inexpensive muslins and cottons can be used extravagantly to great effect, particularly when combined with gently draped valances in a contrasting colour or fabric. Wooden pelmets that follow the architectural lines of the windows define the space very effectively; any piece of hand-carved wood, perhaps painted, can be used instead.

The style of the curtains you choose should depend on the shape, detailing and positioning of the windows. It would be a pity to hide beautiful shutters behind heavy curtains, especially if they are decorated with hand-painted motifs or stencils; the curtains can also block out too much natural light. Narrow windows tend to look better with sill-length curtains; if the window is too wide for its depth, continue curtains to floor level.

More casual than curtains are wide-slatted, wooden Venetians, and cane and bamboo blinds; the latter diffuse the light in familiar stripes. Of the fabric blinds, Roman blinds have a less fussy look than festoon ones, and yet have a gentler line than roller blinds.

Windowseats built into bay or bow windows will be bathed in natural light, take up space that is generally under-used, and can incorporate storage. Add cushions shaped to fit the windowseat, and bolsters for extra comfort. Another way to take advantage of a beautiful view is to draw up an informal circle of chairs in front of a low-silled window.

HOT AND SPICY
In this adobe, (left), a woven Navajo Indian blanket has been used as a curtain against plain plaster walls. The strong light outside permits the use of such contrasts: in colder climates, however, the combination of the bright white and strong colours can look very bleak.

FAMILY GROUP
A comfortable mix of furniture, fabrics and patterns has been created in a plain white room (right): a two-person sofa covered in a flowery chintz in blues and reds which is also used for the curtains, a pair of tartan upholstered chairs with a little round pedestal table, and a Persian-style carpet with pink and red background. The appeal of the room has been strengthened even further by the inclusion of a selection of paintings, some in folk-art style, and objects displayed on every spare bit of flat surface.

PATCHWORKS

*Flinging a patchwork quilt over
a seat (right) is very attractive,
though an heirloom handmade
quilt should be treated more
gently. Here, the patchwork is
machine-made from a wide mix
of fabrics and patterns, and
accompanied by an assortment
of multicoloured cushions.*

EARTH NOTES

*Rich earthy colours, which
complement the patina of the
Windsor chairs, drop-leaf table
and old corner cupboard, have
been chosen to decorate this
room (left). The wooden floor
has been painted mustard yellow
which is picked up in the
geometric curtains. The
traditional hooked rag rug has
faded but the colours and
pattern are still recognisable.*

CROWDED SHELVES
A group of unframed paintings – botanical still-lifes, figures and landscapes look better collected on a mantel shelf (left) than they would hung singly on walls.

A whole ceramic village (right) of honey pots, cookie jars and tea pots are huddled together on a dresser.

The Mexican painter Frida Kahlo collected local ceramic masks and hung them on each side of shelves full of vivid examples of folk art (far right).

PUT TO NEW USE
An unused fireplace (left) now frames a collection of half-glazed Provençal cooking and storage pots. A painted basket of exotic hydrangeas and overblown poppies (above) screens another fireplace.

COUNTRY COLLECTIONS

The imaginative display of a collection of rural objects can set the tone of a room.

● The collection should have a unifying feature, either subject or colour, if it is to look good displayed together.

● Consider the scale of the objects when deciding how to display them. A group of large hats which have a strong graphic shape need space around them and will read from a distance; small finely detailed objects – lace bobbins, for example, or thimbles – need to be viewed from close to, and will look lost if they are too far apart.

● The colour behind a group of objects can make all the difference to the effect: aim for something that contrasts rather than matches otherwise the collection will be lost.

KITCHENS

COUNTRY INGENUITY
At first glance this could be a
kitchen of a hundred years ago
(left) – open fireplace, baskets
and candles hanging from the
ceiling, comfortable wooden
chairs – but closer inspection
reveals modern appliances
cleverly incorporated into the
kitchen units; proof that a
country kitchen does not have
to be old fashioned.

The accoutrements of the
country kitchen (above): jars of
preserved fruits and vegetables,
bunches of fresh herbs, a
selection of dried fungi and
bottles of herb vinegars.

TABLE SENSE
A good sturdy kitchen table (above) provides extra work space and somewhere to relax and enjoy the informality of a chat and a glass of wine with the cook. Even if space is limited, try and fit a small table or counter into the kitchen, particularly for mornings when you can read the newspaper, drink coffee and watch the toast at the same time.

DRIED FLOWERS

Hang flowers upside down in a dry, well-ventilated room, out of direct sunlight, for three weeks to three months – the stems should be crisp. Flowers that dry this way include:
Alchemilla, achillea, astilbe, astrantia, calendula, dahlia, delphinium, gypsophila, hydrangea, lavender, lunaria, statice, nigella, ranunculus and salvia.

Bowls of peaches, bunches of herbs and flowers, jars of preserved fruits, and baskets of tomatoes and eggs in a country kitchen are as important as the colour you choose for the walls or the tiles used on the floor. The idea of the country is one of abundance: acres of wheat, shady orchards, rivers teeming with fish, livestock grazing in idyllic pastoral settings, old barns filled with the new harvest. It's not surprising that the image of the country kitchen is one of delicious aromas of home baking, slow-cooked stews, garden salads and freshly brewed coffee.

The kitchen has always been the heart of the country house, where you can enjoy the crackle of logs in a wood-burning stove, the comfort of scrubbed wood, and the sight of a cat stretching out contentedly. In summer, doors and windows are flung open, the scent of fresh flowers and herbs overwhelms, and produce from the vegetable garden or the local market spills out over the countertops.

Happily, a country-style kitchen is just as obtainable, and can work just as well, in a tiny apartment in Manhattan or London as it does in a farmhouse in Tuscany. It's the positioning of the stove, sink and storage areas that makes a kitchen function efficiently, not high-tech cupboard doors and seamless surfaces. And there is no need to sacrifice the convenience of modern appliances and equipment in a country-style kitchen. A dishwasher or food processor can look at home alongside such traditional country elements as a dresser displaying a collection of milk jugs or a checkered tiled floor.

People tend to congregate in large kitchens, attracted by the informality and buzz of activity that comes with the preparation of meals. A generous-sized kitchen is often not feasible, however, especially in modern apartments. If space is at a premium, consider location carefully; instead of a separate kitchen, it may be better to open up a wall and combine the kitchen and living room, convert a corner of a larger room, or install a small kitchen under the stairs.

The kitchen should always be adjacent to the dining area. Country-style living encourages an easy approach to entertaining, something to be cherished by hosts who work full time and get home just ahead of the guests, yet like to serve up something special. When the family and friends can sit within view of the cook, they can snack on salad ingredients, grate cheese and whisk up egg whites, and – comforted by the sight and smells of the kitchen – are less likely to complain when their dinner is served in the late hours of the evening.

EXTENDED SPACE
Two rooms have been opened into one (left) to create the impression of generous space typical of country kitchens. The table serves as a dividing line between kitchen and living room – it can function as a work surface or a dining table depending on need. Dried flowers hanging from the ceiling in the kitchen area give way to decorative plates hung high on the walls, subtly changing the atmosphere.

COPPER BOTTOMS
An impressive collection of copper pots, gratin dishes, soup pots and jelly moulds are displayed to great effect on hooks and shelves (right). Chefs and serious cooks prefer to use pots made of copper because of the metal's exceptional ability to conduct heat; good quality pots are usually very expensive and are lined with tin or stainless steel, and sometimes with silver.

SURFACES AND TEXTURES

BLUE ON BLUE

Modern appliances and uneven plaster walls in an old country kitchen (above) are unified by the extensive use of blue ceramic tiles. The splash-back that stretches the length of the countertop is tiled in a blue-and-white pattern, which has been repeated on the table, and plain blue is used on the countertop.

PLAIN GOOD LOOKS

The sunlight that floods into this handsome kitchen (right) is filtered through sloping ceiling windows. Tongue-and-groove panelled walls are painted cream, as is the plain custom-built dresser. Great attention has been paid to detail: the carpentry is plain but perfectly finished and the visual interest is provided by texture rather than colour or pattern.

A simple but spectacular splash-back (overleaf) is composed of highly glazed pink and green square tiles set on the diagonal.

Traditional materials – warm reddish-brown quarry tiles, coloured glazed ceramics, slabs of marble or granite, and mellow wood used in cabinets, on the floor, or for countertops – provide a strong basis for a country kitchen. But more modern alternatives, linoleums and stainless steel, for example, have a place here too, and they have the advantage of being easier to maintain.

Purely practical demands should underline decisions about kitchen decoration. Kitchen surfaces need to be resistant to steam, and easy to clean and maintain. Tiles must be laid on a smooth surface; unglazed tiles must be sealed. Paint, whether used on plaster or wood, should have a washable finish, and be either painted or sealed, and you should seal polished wood floors.

Tongue-and-groove walls, which are fairly common in weatherboard houses, are usually painted. If only the dado is made of boards, the upper wall can be treated in a different way; perhaps painted in a slightly paler shade, or wallpapered (with a washable paper). Plaster walls, sometimes finished very smoothly but often left rough, look best with a matt or satin paint finish. If you want a light, bright kitchen, choose soft hues; stronger colours have a more dramatic effect.

Tiles are a favourite hardwearing material used on floors, countertops, and on the walls between the bench and cabinets. Floors of Provençal quarry tiles and black-and-white checkered patterns add a distinctly French flavour. Plain coloured tiles can be laid in geometric patterns – for instance, a red with white and pale green – and tied together with a plain or checkered border. More adventurous are countertops and splash-backs made of colourful glazed tiles from Spain and North Africa decorated with traditional Arabic motifs. Similar designs are found on tiles made in Mexico, but the colours, like the food, are hotter. Hygienic cream ceramic tiles are often associated with restaurants but the long rectangular ones look completely different from the more common large square tiles, and they can be laid in traditional brick patterns. Marble – like terrazzo, granite, slate and stone – is expensive, but will always look good, and makes excellent countertops as well as floors.

For softer, quieter floors, linoleum and vinyl are available in a wide variety of patterns, including many traditional country flooring designs, from the intricate mosaics of Pompeii, through classical Renaissance patterns to simple checks and stripes.

UP-TO-DATE COUNTRY

Modern kitchen cabinets in a pale pearly grey look good with blue knobs and a marble countertop (main picture). Some of the doors on the wall cabinets have been taken off, revealing shelves of china and kitchen containers. The addition of an old pine table and cane-seated chairs provides the country finishing touches.

WOOD AND TILES

Rough timber boards (left) laid horizontally emphasize the long thin window that runs along the tiled countertop.

Wood in various guises (below) – stripped, polished and painted – has been combined with chunky grey and rust quarry tiles, simple red gingham table cloth and rattan-seated chairs.

FLOOR PATTERNS

Tiled floors are universally associated with the country kitchen. Quarry and black-and-white tiles are common but other colour schemes and materials such as linoleum or vinyl can be used. In the simplest patterns, different coloured squares are alternated. However, there are many tile shapes available.

- Prepare the floor according to the manufacturer's instructions – a badly prepared floor can result in bumps or broken tiles.
- Measure the floor and plot your design on graph paper.
- Mark off sections of the floor and work from the centre so that the design is symmetrical down the main axis of the room. Cut border tiles to fit.

FOCAL POINTS

When renovating a kitchen or installing one from scratch, you have the opportunity to plan for efficiency, based on a 'work triangle' drawn between the three main activity areas; food storage, sink and stove. Ideally, the work triangle should not be interrupted by through traffic, especially the route between the stove and the sink, since hot pots and dishes often need to be carried between the two. The most natural – and therefore the most efficient – way of working is from left to right (reversed for left-handed people) with the sink in the centre and the stove on the right: whatever the shape of the work space, the countertop between needs to be a good length because it is the main food preparation area.

All the work areas should have good lighting. Fittings that can be adjusted so you can work without being in your own, or anyone else's shadow are ideal. Combine them with a central, glass-shaded light, which is a traditional choice and still works well for general lighting.

The country look need not be a slavish reproduction of a pre-electric era. A modern reinterpretation incorporates all the time- and space-saving appliances of the high-tech kitchen, but places them in a softer, more human environment. Shiny stainless steel restaurant stoves, built-in ovens and cooking-tops, microwave ovens and barbecue grills can be installed alongside, or instead of, traditional cast-iron stoves. They look equally at ease in an old farmhouse kitchen – complete with checkered tile floor, copper pots, pretty china and bleached pine furniture – as in a natural-hued contemporary country kitchen with white plaster and ceramic tiled walls, streamlined white cabinets, wooden beachtops and furniture designed by Alvar Aalto, the Finnish architect.

The modern appliance can replace the old-fashioned wood- or coal-burning stove in a fireplace, or a handsome reproduction stove that incorporates a water heater can be installed. If you do have a working fireplace in the kitchen it can be equipped with a griddle for grilling (broiling).

Refrigerators and freezers which fit under a bench are available, but have quite limited capacities. Freestanding models can be left alone, built into cabinets or fitted with fascia-board fronts but, if they are particularly large, are better in a pantry or cupboard. Any modern sink can be incorporated into a countertop, or an old-fashioned rectangular butler's sink could be used; it is deeper than most of today's versions and allow plenty of room for washing large pots and pans or laundry.

STOVE POWER

Efficient as modern ovens are, for many the ideal focus of a country kitchen is a cast-iron stove, in this case a classic Aga, which will warm the kitchen and the household water as well as being used for cooking. The large copper extractor hood contributes a special warm glow repeating the colour of the bare bricks behind the stove.

DOUBLE SINK

This pantry sink and draining board (right) are covered in copper, and the high curved taps (faucets), which allow large pots to fit underneath, are both elegant and practical. A second sink, in a pantry or corner of the kitchen, is a convenient place to wash vegetables, cool sauces, or keep shellfish alive until needed.

FURNITURE

KEYNOTE KITCHEN FURNISHINGS
A butcher's block (above), a settle or a simple, solid table (right)
can each, individually, set the country tone in a kitchen.

The favoured kitchen of today has built-in cabinets and appliances. But the country style is a more laissez-faire approach, mixing new and old pieces of furniture, using freestanding stoves, plain or painted dressers laden with pretty china, corner cabinets and marble- or granite-top work centres.

Streamlined units are by no means out of place in the country kitchen, but the introduction of a butcher's block or a painted dresser softens the look of the room. Existing built-in kitchens can be updated quickly and cheaply by changing the cabinet doors and worktop. Replacing melamine with wooden doors, or a Formica countertop with one made of beech or slate, using more subtle lighting and laying checkered black-and-white linoleum flooring can turn an ordinary-looking kitchen into a room with a definite country character.

One of the great advantages of using individual items of furniture is that good-quality pieces are an investment and can be taken with you if you move house. And it can be a more sympathetic way of treating old rooms; rather than ripping out architectural features, and thus destroying the atmosphere, in order to fit built-in units, individual pieces can be planned around the room's features.

Furniture makers nowadays are producing some beautiful hand-crafted dressers and sideboards; oiled or limed woods or muted lacquers, the favoured finishes, are perfect in a country kitchen. Preparation tables that incorporate butchers' blocks, drawer storage and pull-out shelves work best in good-sized kitchens, although small pull-out trolley versions solve space problems in the smallest kitchens.

Even if space is at a premium, a small table and one or two dining chairs are invaluable in a kitchen. As well as adding extra work space, breakfast and informal meals can be eaten in the kitchen, and visitors have a place to sit and talk to the cook. Marble-topped bistro tables, folding garden furniture and stylish 1930s wrought-iron pieces are unconventional but successful choices.

REVIVING FURNITURE

The warm wood tones of chairs, tables and chests that are crucial to the country look are often concealed beneath layers of old and unattractive paint. Stripping, light repair and wax polishing can reveal a beautiful piece of furniture. However, before deciding to restore an old chair or chest found in the loft it is worth considering a number of points.

• 'Antique' and 'distressed' paint surfaces are now very fashionable. In the right context even a battered, painted kitchen chair can look very beautiful so do not consign it to the stripper without cleaning it up and taking another look first.
• Do not waste time restoring pieces of furniture that are badly put together or made of inferior wood. A look at the underside of a chair or the inside of a drawer can often give a clue.
• Do not waste time on pieces that are riddled with woodworm. Inspect them very carefully, especially around the feet.
• If you are going to carry out the restoration yourself, start with a modest piece.

BRIGHT AND PRACTICAL
Solid practical furniture – a
pine table, Windsor chairs and
settle – make a sunny corner of
a country kitchen a good place
for children to do homework or
paint under a watchful eye.

PERFECT PIECES
A chest of drawers (above),
brought into the kitchen and
given a new marble top, has
useful deep drawers which are
practical for storing table linen
and awkwardly shaped,
specialized kitchen equipment
that is not in everyday use.

A comfortable antique
folding chair (above right) has
found a place by the fireside.

A long, polished refectory-
type table (right) is flanked by
bench seats, on which you could
fit an army.

FOOD STORAGE

The old-fashioned country kitchen incorporated walk-in larders, many with stone floors and walls to keep food chilled. Ideally situated on a cool side of the house, the larder would have had louvred doors which allowed air to circulate: pierced tin panels, wooden latticework and slatted shelves are traditional substitutes. Dishes were kept in a separate pantry, and it was here on the traditional marble countertop that pastry was made.

If there's space in a modern house or apartment a small larder-cum-pantry, situated on an outer wall and well ventilated, is a good addition. Stacked with shelves of bottled fruits and vegetables and jars of home-made jams and chutneys, preserved hams and fish hung from ceiling racks along with bunches of drying herbs, the larder stores all the fruits of the harvest.

HERB OILS AND VINEGARS

The scents of summer herbs can be preserved for use in cooking and for dressing vegetables and salads throughout the winter by preparing herb-flavoured oils and vinegars.

● Pick herbs for flavouring oils and vinegars first thing in the morning just after the dew has dried so that the essential oils are at their most concentrated. All parts of the herbs can be used: leaves, flowers and seeds.

● Use good quality wine or cider vinegar and olive oil (best for strongly flavoured herbs like tarragon or basil) or milder oils such as sunflower.

● Fill a clean, clear bottle with bruised herbs and pour over the oil or vinegar. Seal the top.

● Leave on a sunny window-sill for two weeks. If you wish, strain the oil or vinegar and put in a fresh herb sprig.

In smaller kitchens beautiful jars and bottles can be displayed on open shelves or in glass-fronted wall-hung cabinets or dressers, along with collections of china and glass. Preserving jars of different types and sizes can also be used to store dry ingredients such as sugar, rice, pasta and pulses when they are to be displayed on open shelves.

Everyday ingredients like herbs and spices are usually kept near at hand; salt in traditional wooden salt boxes hung on the wall or salt 'pigs'; herbs and spices in old-fashioned racks or good-looking glass jars – preferably dark ones to preserve the strength of the herbs; olive oil in attractive corked bottles. Bunches of drying herbs and flowers can be hung from the rafters and herbs tied into wreaths hanging on the kitchen wall ready for use when needed are a traditional kitchen feature.

COUNTRY STORE
The country harvest (far left) – preserved vegetables in old-fashioned glass-topped preserving jars – is evocative enough to be set out in order to enrich the imagination.

The buttery at Coffin House in Newbury, Massachusetts (left), has been turned into a model pantry displaying beautiful bowls, baskets and utensils on long shelves.

STORE HOUSE
Sausages hanging from the rafters (below), tomatoes and other preserves on rudimentary shelves, and crocks of wine and olives are kept in this larder. Alongside a collection of beautiful half-glazed earthenware, the owners have placed a classically shaped urn in a niche in the wall, perfectly understanding the connection between food and classicism.

RICH HARVEST

A pine dresser (left) is groaning under the weight of bottled fruits, vegetables, preserves, sauces and vinegars. Glass preserving jars with metal caps or glass clamp tops have a beauty all of their own, rendering even the most mundane pickled onions beautiful and worthy of display. Old metal covers, scales, jelly moulds and pretty dishes add to the delight of the dresser and beneath it apples and potatoes are stored in lovely baskets.

HANDMADE BOXES

Instead of using tins or, later, plastic containers, the American Shaker communities made oval boxes of pine or maple in all sizes to store all manner of household and workshop items including food. The boxes were either left plain, showing off the beauty of the wood they used, or painted in earth colours – yellow, rust red, olive green or muddy blue.

KITCHEN EQUIPMENT

FUNCTIONAL AND DECORATIVE
Good quality kitchen equipment is almost always worthy of display,
whether on shelves (above) or hung on a rack (left).

Kitchen equipment and utensils, particularly those, such as copper pots and pans and moulds, which are naturally decorative, are generally stored on view in the country kitchen. Pans can be placed on high shelves, hung on the wall beside the stove or kept in tiered cast iron or wooden pan stands. Cooking spoons, colanders and ladles can be suspended on hooks near the preparation area or a rail can be attached to the wall or to the underside of a cupboard over the countertop with butcher's hooks to carry the *batterie de cuisine*. Keep wooden spoons, whisks and rolling pins in a tall pottery jar near the stove.

Mixing bowls and other pottery are often displayed on open shelves, dressers, or traditional plate racks which have a bar across the front of each shelf to support the plates and bowls. If shelf space is limited, large bowls look very attractive stacked one inside the other and kept in a spare corner of the preparation area. Plates can be displayed in wooden draining racks as well as on the wall.

There is no need to throw out modern stainless steel kitchen equipment when creating a country style kitchen. It will fit in very well, but it is worth looking out for old pieces of equipment such as enamel colanders or flour bins (useful for storing bread), decorative tins, scales, china moulds and terrines, cutlery trays, wire egg baskets, cookie cutters or bread boards which all serve both a practical and a decorative purpose. French Provencal or Italian half-glazed cooking pots and storage jars look very beautiful as do crackle-glaze pottery or spongeware.

The finishing touches are paintings or prints of domestic animals, vegetables or fruit, old painted signs and baskets of all different shapes and sizes which can be suspended from the rafters or displayed on open shelves.

WEIGH AND WASH
Pride of place should always be awarded to a set of brass and iron scales as lovely as these (right).

Cheese draining moulds can be put to new use as cutlery drainers (below).

DISPLAY SHELVES
A dark wood rack with high restraining bars (far left) is a surprisingly capacious means of storing large gratin dishes, soufflé dishes, mixing bowls and pretty everyday china.

Part of the appeal of a kitchen dresser (left) is the unifying effect it has on any multiplicity of objects.

In an unusual kitchen with a pitched roof, storage space — reached via a compact spiral staircase — has been built under the rafters for large items such as baskets.

COUNTRY DINING

EASY COMFORT
Dusky rose-tinted walls (left)
provide a strong backdrop for
the play between the white used
on the woodwork and the dark
furniture and details. The table
has been placed widthways to
take full advantage of the
daylight, the sideboard doubles
as storage and serving space
and spare chairs are kept
against the walls.

A corner cabinet in rich
wood (above) is accompanied by
a painted plate-rack, set on the
floor to carry large dishes.

The famous yellow dining room created by the French Impressionist Claude Monet in his home at Giverny, in Normandy, is the epitome of the country style. It has a robust simplicity, is designed for convenience as well as beauty, and it conveys the impression of warmth and comfort. A long room with two sets of French windows along one side and an internal door opening on to the kitchen, it is bathed in natural light; as if to emphasize this, the walls are painted in soft tones of yellow, a colour much favoured in country dining rooms everywhere. The practical red-and-white square floor tiles are laid on the diagonal, with a reddish Oriental rug under the table providing both visual and textural contrast. The long table is placed in the centre of the room, and is covered in a utilitarian pale yellow oilcloth. The painted chairs with rush seats and blue-and-white cushions are typical of the region, they have beautiful fanned backs, proof that country-style does not have to be plain. The walls

are lined with part of the painter's collection of subtly coloured Japanese woodcuts. Oriental porcelain is displayed on the walls and in two large painted dressers with glazed upper doors.

The French have a well-known and distinctive passion for food. Their dining areas are marked with the same stamp, and throughout the country there are common themes. Walls are usually painted in whites or creams, in the yellows favoured by Monet, or in closely related soft peaches and oranges. Stronger accent colours are introduced in plates and flowers, in the careful use of patterned fabrics in seat covers, tablecloths and curtains, and often in checkered floor tiles.

In a typical white-walled French country dining room, the table may be covered with an old linen cloth edged with lace, and laid with the palest green napkins, white china, beautiful handblown wine and water glasses, an old silver cruet set and low glass vases of lilies of the valley; chairs are

TIMELESS STYLE
Claude Monet's yellow dining room at Giverny (far left) is conveniently sited next door to the kitchen. The table is set with porcelain designed by the painter and the country furniture has been painted to match the walls.

Two built-in seats (left) and some unmatched chairs in another house in Normandy surround a large square scrubbed table in an uninterrupted corner.

WINDOW SEAT
A long narrow table (below) combined with a window seat and a bench makes good sense in this dining area tucked in at the side of a kitchen in northern Italy.

The height of the room has been emphasized by the way the red and dark blue frescoes have been concentrated on the ceiling. Copper moulds and pots hang on the walls above the locally made solid pine cupboard.

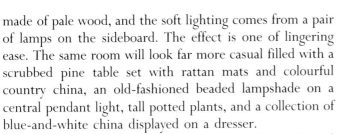

made of pale wood, and the soft lighting comes from a pair of lamps on the sideboard. The effect is one of lingering ease. The same room will look far more casual filled with a scrubbed pine table set with rattan mats and colourful country china, an old-fashioned beaded lampshade on a central pendant light, tall potted plants, and a collection of blue-and-white china displayed on a dresser.

Another French approach is to strip panelled walls and built-in glazed cabinets or paint them all a traditional blue-green. Combined with a round paisley-covered table, painted high-backed chairs with rush seats and pale green cushions, and gilt-framed paintings and mirrors, the result is a dining room that is elegant, visually interesting and comfortable to linger in.

Whether the overall effect is rustic or elegant, in all these country-style dining rooms the emphasis is on comfort, on the natural groupings and easy combination of objects, rather than a contrived imposition of style.

BASICALLY BEAUTIFUL
In an English room with a
beamed ceiling, rough plaster
walls and quarry tiled floor (top
left) fine country furniture has
been arranged around a
fireplace. The furniture has
been chosen as much for beauty
as function.

A folding table (bottom left)
with ornate black-and-gold
chairs is the focal point of the
dining room in this eighteenth-
century New Hampshire house.
In one corner a cabinet has
been built in to store table linen,
cutlery, china and glasses. The
great fireplace holds a collection
of antique fire-irons and copper
jugs and pots.

With bare brick walls a
round table covered with a
checked cloth and gingham
curtains, this Dutch dining
room is the essence of simplicity.

COUNTRY ELEGANCE
The soft yellow of this panelled room reflects the sunlight streaming in through the open door; the shade chosen has none of the relentless cheerfulness that is sometimes associated with yellow. The fine detailing of the panelling and cupboards harmonizes with the elegant Windsor chairs.

FAKING A DADO
A simple way to add interest to modern apartments and decorate in country style without cluttering the room is to create a dado effect.

• Hang heavy embossed paper on the dado area before painting.

• Decorate the dado areas with a special paint finish, such as *trompe-l'oeil* panelling or marbling. Always seal finishes.

• Use a stronger colour on the dado than that on the upper walls; such as rusty red with cream, or deep blue with a paler shade.

• Mark the top edge of the dado with a straight edge of masking tape before painting.

• Hand paint the edge with a fine brush – you must mark the dado line before painting.

• Define the top edge of the dado with a border pattern – perhaps a bold black-and-white geometric or simply a stripe.

LOCATION

GOOD POSITIONS
*A dining area decorated in Arts and Crafts style (left) takes up one
side of a large kitchen. The dining table in a South Carolina house
(above) stands in a corner of the living room.*

For purely practical reasons the dining room area should be located close to the kitchen. Many modern homes don't have space for a separate dining room; instead, meals may be eaten at a table in the living room or even in the kitchen – or, indeed, in both. A wide hall or landing can double as a dining area, and a balcony or verandah may be used in hot weather.

In many older houses the kitchen and dining area are physically separated by a wall of double-sized, floor-to-ceiling cupboards and drawers, allowing access from both

sides. This is a good-looking and convenient place to store china and glassware, and often incorporates a dumb waiter. Other ways to separate the two areas are with a low counter that also provides storage space, a pair of back-to-back cupboards, a centrally placed marble or stone buffet table, or an internal window that allows additional light into both areas. A change of floor surfaces – such as a large rug under the table and chairs, or tiles giving way to wood – or a different wall treatment can also be used to signify the change of use from the kitchen to the dining area.

FURNITURE

AGED SPLENDOUR
Character can be introduced into a dining room as effectively with beautifully curved chair backs (top) displaying the patina of age as with an antique cupboard painted in strong colours and traditional patterns.

AN ASSURED MIX
Pieces of simple, old wooden country furniture – locally made chairs, a big dark cabinet full of blue-and-white china and a blanket box – have been chosen for their plain good looks as well as their usefulness.

The shape and style of the table and other furniture affect the look of the room. A round, bleached oak table with a set of carved wood chairs will be more formal than a long scrubbed pine table and Windsor chairs, or a medieval-looking oak table in front of a settle with unmatched rush-seated chairs around the other sides.

Round tables have a reputation for being the ideal for dining since they are more democratic and make it easier to converse with those opposite you. But in fact the most common shape for a country dining table is a rectangle; it is the simplest kind of table to make and takes up less space. And indeed there is something more enjoyable, even ritualistic, about sitting at a long table, paying attention to your immediate neighbours yet straining to hear snatches of conversation from the opposite end, passing along dishes of food and trying to get someone to hand you the wine. Where space is limited, choose drop-leaf tables and those which can be extended for entertaining.

The chairs should be chosen for comfort as well as for good looks. Simple wooden chairs with rush seats, Thonet bentwoods, carved wood frames with upholstered seats, *faux* bamboo chairs, Windsors, high-backed Swedish chairs with blue-and-white checked seats and mahogany Sheratons with gold decoration all have a place in the country-style dining room. Styles can be mixed, which works as long as they have a common visual theme, such as material, shape, colour and size, and hard seats can be softened with slim cushions attached to the chair back with ties.

Other seating can include furniture that has been designed originally for use outdoors – such as cast-iron bistro chairs, comfortable Lloyd Loom chairs, fine-lined black metal chairs with cream cushions, and fold-up-wooden- and steel-framed chairs – as well as benches that can be pushed under the table when not in use, ornate wooden settles, and upholstered banquettes.

A sideboard is a traditional, and useful, piece of dining-room furniture. Cutlery and napkins, glasses and china are stored in its cupboards and drawers, and condiments, fruits, cheeses and wine are left on top. Food and serving dishes can be displayed on a narrow buffet table or a pair of semi-circular tables, and dressers or open shelves will hold beautiful pieces of china and glassware. Where space is limited or the room is also used for other activities, built-in cabinets provide ample storage space; they can be angled on a diagonal across a corner, and the upper doors glazed to show off collections of pottery and china.

COUNTRY CHINA

DISPLAYING CHINA

Collections of colourful country plates, cups, jugs and bowls are as effective in giving warmth to a dining room as books are to a living room.

- Traditional dressers with deep shelves often have a narrow strip of wood fixed a little way forward of the back of the shelf to prevent plates ranged along the back from sliding down and breaking. A similar device can be used to hold plates on any row of shelves.
- Jugs, cups and mugs – so long as the handles are quite sound and in no danger of breaking – can be displayed hung by small butcher's hooks on rails, or hung from cup hooks screwed into the underside of shelves.
- Plates, bowls and dishes can be supported in a rack with a bar across the front of each shelf, leaning forward rather than leaning back.
- Shelf edges can be decorated by tacking lengths of lace or lacy cut-out paper along the front of each shelf.

Traditional ceramic dishes have a timeless quality; there is much to be said for picking up one or two local examples every time you go on vacation, you can mix them together on a table successfully. The composition of the raw materials, the glazes and decoration may differ slightly from region to region, but all over the world shapes repeat the fluid lines of classical pieces: beautifully curved bowls, ridged dishes, graceful pitchers and large round and oval platters.

Brown half-glazed earthenware is used for cooking utensils, such as French gratin dishes and the Moroccan tagine. Serving dishes and bowls may be decorated, often by hand: sometimes the glaze is combed or spattered, or motifs and patterns traditional to the region are used. Colours are earthy – reddish browns, mustards, yellows, creams – or brighter greens and blues, and are handled in different ways, according to the region. Quimperware from Brittany, for example, has a cream background and colourful hand-painted antique designs. Brighter colours and Moorish motifs are characteristic of Mexican pottery. In Columbia pottery is glazed and fired twice, and the result is a very dark brown dish which feels more like wood.

COUNTRY COLOURS
The nineteenth-century love of decoration is evident in a sculptured line-up of milk jugs (far left) displayed on a window sill in Normandy.

Blue-and-white china forms the basis of a pretty collection (left) displayed to great advantage on a mellow-coloured pine dresser. Contrasting pinks and yellows add life to the composition.

The garden is an enduring theme of country china. Pieces (below) from antique shops and markets are mixed and matched to great effect. The tableware on the lower shelves of the dresser was popular in the 1930s and 1940s.

PLATES AND DRESSERS
An eclectic collection of china (top, far left) – creamware baskets, cabbage-leaf platters and plates embossed with grapes, peaches and flowers have been displayed, closely packed, in a narrow, glass-fronted cupboard.

A set of display shelves (top left) has been fitted across an odd-shaped corner and edged with lengths of lace in four different patterns which enhance the delicate charm of a pretty collection of tea and coffee sets and glasses in different colours.

A large traditional pine dresser (below, far left) holds a collection of 20th-century china in strong colours and patterns.

An old built-in cupboard (below left) holds stacks of dinner and dessert plates. The antiquity of the paintings and pieces of paper stuck on the back of the door imbues them with a faded attractiveness.

Old blue-and-white designs (right) and china with botanical themes never go out of fashion. Patterns need not be matching; indeed, a table set with china of different designs but common colours can look charming.

DINING ROOM DETAILS

Tablecloths of lace are something of a cliché, but they do look beautiful over a long pale undercloth and set with old silver cutlery and pretty plates. Starched white damask always looks appropiate but because it requires a lot of attention it is best reserved for special meals. Plain or patterned oilcloths that can be wiped down are practical, attractive and a good choice for everyday family occasions.

In a typical Swedish dining room, with walls painted the intense blue-white widely used and a white table and chairs, often the only colour comes from the blue-and-white checked seats and matching blinds. Red-and-white check is a quintessential country favourite, too, for tablecloths, napkins, and even cushions and curtains. Stronger patterns – batiks, paisleys and brightly coloured Provençal cottons, for instance – are often used as undercloths with short white or contrasting cloths.

When setting a table for a special meal add low vases of flowers picked straight from the garden. More unusual are branches of mistletoe and hawthorn berries, trailing sprays of honeysuckle or ivy, bowls of fresh herbs, still-lives of wooden fruits and vegetables, and brightly coloured bowls or baskets filled with ready-grown annuals, snowdrops, crocuses or primroses.

Lighting should always be soft and discreet. A central pendant lamp which can be lowered so that its bulb is out of sight illuminates the table without causing glare; this is a good solution for family dining rooms, particularly if the table is used for purposes other than meals and a good source of general lighting is needed. Place table lamps on a sideboard for supplementing lighting.

More romantic is a country-style candelabrum, such as a two-tiered Shaker version, hung over the table. Groups of thin candlesticks can be set on the table but they should be arranged so that people sitting on the opposite side of the table are not obscured. Wall sconces holding candles are an almost forgotten form of lighting – simple tin ones are charming – and if there is a working fireplace, flickering firelight enhances the mood.

SETTING TABLES
A tartan blanket (left) is an unexpected but striking covering for a long refectory table set with odd-patterned blue-and-white plates and white candles in tall unmatched silver and low china candlesticks.

One end of a table laid with a pale green oilskin cloth (below) has been set with an elaborate candelabrum, everyday china and unusual table mats.

FLICKERING LIGHT
A Shaker-style candelabrum – delicate metal arms supporting simple dipped candles – is an appealing alternative to an overhead light if you desire soft light on the dining table.

BEDROOMS
AND
BATHROOMS

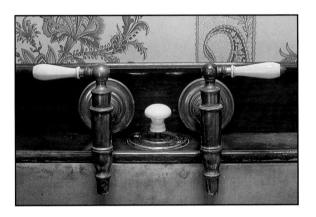

CASUAL COMBINATIONS
A traditional red and white
patchwork quilt on an antique
wooden bedstead is the focal
point of this country bedroom
(left). The casual way patterns
are combined, colours are mixed
and assorted objects chosen are
typical of the country style:
walls are covered in a stylized
Shaker design, the wooden
mantelpiece has been decorated
to resemble exotically veined
marble, and the painting over
the mantel is in a bold folk art
tradition.

A bathroom feature to be
treasured is a pair of old-
fashioned brass taps (above)
with lever handles.

The country bedroom is a natural retreat filled with your most personal possessions – great-grand-mother's sampler, children's paintings, eccentric collections of hairbrushes or perfume bottles – and decorated in your favourite colours. It is a room seen mainly at night-time, usually under artificial lights, and early in the day. One approach, therefore, is to use colours that look mellow in lamplight and wonderful in the morning light, which is filtered by curtains or blinds and falls in patterns across the floor when you wake up.

White, cream and pastels are versatile choices for a bedroom, and a good basis for a number of different country looks. The French add lots of linen edged with crochet and lace, beautiful old wooden furniture, and filmy curtains of fine muslin. Beams and structural timbers are left exposed in old English country cottages, and much is made of the play between painted or colour-washed plaster and dark wood; a similiar effect can be created by treating door and window frames and skirting boards with a dark stain. Rocking chairs, strongly patterned quilted bedcovers and rag rugs are traditional additions in America.

The Shakers sometimes added stencilled borders or covered plain walls and floor with delicate stylized designs, often based on nature or such motifs as stars or diamonds, and made beautiful patchwork quilts to cover the bed. Carl Larsson, the Swedish painter and designer working in the early years of this century, also used stencilled patterns to decorate his house. First, he painted the floorboards cream, then drew on motifs, such as hearts and berries, in green and red or in blues, using the same colours to outline the window frames and skirting boards. Ready-made stencils are widely available and easy to use; printed borders give a similar, although more 'manufactured', look.

In the French farmhouse, stronger colours – such as pinks, ochres and greens – are characteristically used with patterned fabrics and polished or stripped woods. Clear blues, yellows and even reds – colours that are especially favoured in hotter climates, such as in the southern United States and in Australia – emphasize the smoothness or roughness of the plaster, the ribs of tongue-and-groove boards, the flatness of a papered wall, and so create great textural interest.

A bedroom papered in a tiny flower print is one of the classic English country looks. Miniature rosebuds on a pale pink background, bunches of violets tied with ribbon, linear patterns of daffodils, and dainty baskets of cottage garden

IMAGINATIVE COLOURING
Instead of staining the ceiling
beams and wall timbers as is
usual, the owners of this French
bedroom (top, far left) painted
them a green-blue. The effect is
much lighter, yet retains the
natural charm of the original.

In another bedroom in the
same house (below, far left) the
beams are a dusky orange and
the furnishings have been
chosen to harmonize.

Here, too (left), the
traditional treatment of the
ceiling – leaving the wood bare
or painting it white or cream –
has been eschewed in favour of
a turquoise-green. This makes
much of the structural timbers
without casting a gloom, as
bare wood may have done, and
cuts down the glare from the
sun-drenched plaster walls.

blooms are combined with white woodwork, painted or cane furniture, white-on-white bedcovers and pretty cotton lawn curtains. It is a romantic look that suits small bedrooms, and particularly attic rooms.

The Victorian designer and writer William Morris introduced more stylized patterns for wallpapers and fabrics based on country themes and inspired by traditional Eastern patterns. His designs using roses and lilies, birds and pomegranates, jasmine and honeysuckle – many of which are still produced – are well suited to more formal country bedrooms. Bolder floral patterns are much more popular in America than they are in Europe, and they are used in a distinctive New World way. Big fresh flower designs, usually on white, cover the walls, bedspreads are traditional folk quilt designs, and strongly patterned floor coverings such as checkered tiles or linoleum are used. Alternatively, floral chintz curtains and bedcover are combined with plain walls, bare floorboards and a rag rug.

Wooden floors – whether laid in short strips or long boards, or as parquet – can be painted or varnished, polished or bleached. The rougher textured carpets, and sisal or coir matting, which are slightly ticklish underfoot, are more traditional in a country bedroom than luxurious carpet laid wall to wall (although pale carpets covered with rugs are *very* comfortable and do not look out of place). The harder, colder-feeling flooring materials – such as stone, marble, tiles and bricks – can feel quite warm in more temperate, even cold, regions if underfloor heating is installed. Whatever type of flooring is used, rugs add softness, and areas of colour and pattern.

LIGHT AND AIRY
Simplicity is the keyword in this Australian bedroom (far left). The tongue-and-groove boards lining the walls, the wicker chair and blanket box, the heavy crochet cushion and the cotton floor rug are all white, and just a little colour is introduced in the ticking bedcover. What draws the eye are the French windows and the sensible but decorative waist-high balustrade, which have been outlined in dark green, making a frame for the garden view.

LACE ARCH
Bare wooden floorboards and plain plaster walls (left) are a good background for an eighteenth-century American arched tester bedstead covered with lace and a beautiful quilted and appliquéd bedspread.

MAJESTIC COUNTRY
In a generous bedroom in a wooden holiday house (oveleaf), the bed has been made up with crisp white sheets and pillowslips, an embroidered Spanish fringed shawl and a Welsh-quilted bedcover. A sofa by the window takes advantage of the sun and the view. Colours have been kept deliberately muted, and, in the form of a beautiful painted blanket box, pattern is confined to the lower levels of the room in order to show off the linear patterns created by the wooden walls, rafters and ceiling.

BEDS

WITTY AND WISE
A lovely antique bed (above)
has been happily transformed
by the elegant canopy that falls
in generous folds from the
sloping ceiling. The extravagant
– and exclusive – use of such a
sensible country fabric as blue-
and-white gingham is a clever
and wholly successful ploy.

A beautiful old wooden bedstead – whether of a distinctive wood such as oak, fine-grained·like walnut or cherrywood, or a good-quality durable pine – is the focal point of the country bedroom, and if you're lucky enough to have one it is to be treasured. The patina built up over decades cannot be faked, but it's worth stripping down a painted bed and, if the wood is good-looking, it can then be treated with wax; otherwise the bed can be given a decorative paint finish, such as antiquing, staining, stencilling or lacquering.

The style of wooden beds varies from four posters and canopy beds to those with plain headboards, perhaps ornamented with turned newel posts. Four posters used to be draped with heavy fabrics designed to keep out the light and the air, but by the mid-nineteenth century the idea of well-ventilated bedrooms had caught on and lighter muslins, fine cottons and lace were favoured. Bed – and window – drapes in a country bedroom should always be kept simple; ruffles and the like are out of place.

Traditional iron and brass bedsteads are fairly easy to find, and reproductions are widely available. The iron is usually painted black or dark green, because the dark colours emphasize the decorative lines of the bed, but white can look good against very pale walls.

Many antique beds are extremely uncomfortable, and they are often shorter than modern beds. In some old beds, the mattress (stuffed with straw or feathers) was supported by ropes interlaced through holes in the bed rails. The side rails of these, and most wooden and iron bedsteads can be replaced by ones made to measure, and slatted bases substituted for uncomfortable rope or spring ones.

In European farmhouses beds are traditionally built into alcoves, often close to a fireplace. The bed is raised on a base, which can be used for storage, and the alcove is framed with decorative panels and sometimes enclosed by light curtains. In the Scandinavian countries, panels are often painted white with beading highlighted in a strong blue, red or green; further south the wood is usually left unpainted. A built-in bed is a good solution if space is at a premium, and works well in children's rooms.

Modern bases and mattresses also have a place in the country bedroom, dressed up with a beautiful quilt or a traditional woven blanket. A hand-carved bedhead found in an antique shop or home made, a piece of embroidery or patchwork quilt hung on the wall in lieu of a headboard, or a pile of handsome cushions add the country flavour.

BLUE AND WHITE
Big blue-and-white checks are
used as canopy and bedcover for
this four-poster in Casey's
Farmhouse on Rhode Island.
The original canopy was
probably hung with heavier
drapes to protect the sleeper
from the night air, an idea that
went out of fashion in the
mid-nineteenth century.
   A strong blue defines a
built-in box bed in a fisherman's
cottage on the coast of Brittany.
This type of bed is particularly
useful in a children's room
where space is at a premium.
Bunks can be incorporated as
well as single beds, and it
provides a great deal of privacy.

BEAUTIFUL BEDS

The dark, elegant lines and understated beauty of a lovely Empire-shaped metal bed (left), ornamented with cut-out arrows, stands out against the white-washed plaster walls and quarry-tiled floor. A cork-screw legged table and an eighteenth-century Italian painting provide the minimum of detail necessary.

The polished sophistication of the carved wooden bedstead (above) contrasts with tongue-and-groove walls, which have been stained an unusual pinkish-brown.

BEDHEADS

A lovely bedhead can define the character of a bedroom. There are many ready-made ones available but a less orthodox option can be just as effective.

● A frame made of carved wood – perhaps lengths of decorative moulding or a back piece rescued from a broken sideboard – can be screwed into the bedbase or attached directly to the wall behind.

● A patchwork or embroidered quilt can be suspended on a wooden towel rail attached to the wall above the bed.

● A simple canopy can be constructed using wide bamboo poles attached to the bedbase; drape it with a light muslin.

BED-LINEN

SIMPLE LUXURY
A white iron bedstead (left) is draped with white bed-linen resplendent with lace and an old white counterpane. Using sheets and pillowslips decorated with antique lace, which can readily be found in markets and secondhand shops, has turned this New York bedroom into a country boudoir.

The white-on-white technique used on this bedcover (below left) is called Welsh quilting, sewn here in a diamond pattern with a double-scallop edge. The high bedhead and matching wardrobe have unusual crossed-over-tops, almost neo-Gothick in style.

BRAZEN PATTERN
In this eighteenth-century New Hampshire bedroom (right) an almost overwhelming combination of different patterns has been carried off with typical assurance. The bold red, white and brown patchwork on the tester bed dominates the room, against a background of stylized fine blue floral wallpaper, crewel-work curtains and geometric and striped rugs.

In the quintessential country bedroom, the bed is covered with an heirloom quilt. The choice is wide and includes woven bedcovers of homespun wools, elaborate quilts made of patchwork, beautiful appliqué covers and the strongly coloured Jacquard coverlets that were woven on the early mechanized looms and were popular in the nineteenth century.

The art of the patchwork quilt reached its high point in eighteenth- and nineteenth-century America. Quilts were made of tiny diamonds and hexagons, and big alternating squares. They were cut out of plain and patterned cottons, wools and silks; in subtle shades, primaries or bold geometrics; and sewn in curved snaking patterns, stars, flower and animal shapes, geometrics and wide stripes. Once completed, the patchwork was interlined and backed, then over-stitched in such shapes as diamonds and squares or patterns printed on the patches.

Quilting was also used on plain cottons and satins and, more elaborately, to outline detailed patterned fabrics. Old patchwork quilts are available in antique shops specializing in folk art, but they are expensive. Making your own is possible, if time-consuming; simpler quilts may not have quite the charm of hand-made ones, but they can at least be sewn on a machine.

Dramatic appliqué bedcovers can be made by handstitching or machining on to them patterns cut from printed fabrics; large acanthus or lilies, for instance, on a handsome base fabric such as heavy linen, fine cotton or a softly coloured velvet. Many old appliqué quilts have very detailed patterns with all the features on each flower, or other image, constructed from tiny pieces of different coloured and textured fabrics. Exquisite Spanish shawls embroidered in satin stitch, cream Indian wools decorated in colourful crewel work, and blankets crocheted in white or cream cotton also make perfect coverlets for a country-style bedroom.

Crisp snow-white cotton or creamy linen sheets are more appropiate in a country bedroom than the coloured and patterned bed-linen available today. New linen sheets are very expensive, but you can still find beautiful old sheets and pillowcases in second-hand shops. Linen lasts a long time and it tends to look better as it ages; the disadvantage is that it needs to be starched and ironed. Good quality cotton, preferably percale, is an excellent alternative.

STORAGE

The handsome armoire in the French country bedroom was often the most highly prized, and valuable, object in the householder's possession, and such a piece of furniture will always be the centre-piece of the room that contains it. Leave wardrobes, chests of drawers and cupboards in good woods unpainted; otherwise it is usually most appropriate to use soft colours such as blue-green or pale turquoises, with details picked out in contrasting shades or in gold.

Often, there is not enough space in a modern bedroom for free-standing wardrobes, and built-in closets are preferred. The Shakers used fine woods to build whole walls of cupboards and drawers with the minimum of fuss; plain-framed doors and unornamented drawer fronts. Sleek-looking modern closets can be given a country look with the addition of fine beading and beautiful old handles and locks; they work best if painted the same shade as the walls or given a distressed paint finish.

Wooden blanket boxes and upholstered ottomans serve the double purpose of providing storage and seating. Ottomans can be covered in heavy striped or floral fabric, or with tapestries or old kilims.

HIDDEN BENEFITS
This neat white-on-white wall on closets and drawers (above) has been shaped to fit into a sloping bedroom wall – common to many country bedrooms – and great attention has been paid to finishing details.

Every inch of space around an attic window (right) has been utilized for storage. The drawers and cupboards support and surround a cosy window seat, with comfortable cushions covered in floral printed cotton.

CUPBOARDS AND CHESTS
A rustic cupboard (left) has
been built into an awkward
corner under the stairs. Made
of unmatched boards, it is
finished with black iron hinges,
and a small triangular shelf just
big enough for a vase of flowers.
   Black and cream hearts,
flowers and cats decorate a
blanket box (above left). This
type of light, rhythmical design
was a favourite American
colonial treatment.
   Heavy wooden furniture can
look heavy and out of balance
with the rest of a room. Painting
this otherwise ordinary wardrobe
(above) makes it seem lighter
and more elegant.

BEDROOM DETAILS

Bright lights have little place in the country bedroom. Lighting that recalls soft candle- or firelight is more in keeping with the atmosphere. Bedside reading lights can be antique oil lamps (modernized with electricity), candlestick lamps with black shades, generous ceramic bases, or even sleek, modern, low-voltage tungsten halogen lamps. A small antique table, miniature chest of drawers or stool can be used as a bedside table, which should be just large enough to hold a lamp, a book and perhaps a telephone.

To complete the bedroom, choose the kind of objects that embody the timeless charm of the country style; collections of baskets, a wooden-framed mirror, samplers, antique, lace-trimmed nightdresses, paintings of birds and fruit, duck decoys, antique pitchers, bowls of freshly picked flowers, a rattan-seat chair.

FUNCTION AND BEAUTY
In most old houses, fireplaces were built in every room in the house. Preserved for decorative effect rather than practical considerations in this bedroom (far left), the fireplace is piled high with dried flowers. When the nights get colder, it is worth lighting the fire and enjoying the flickering flames.

SHAKER ELEGANCE
A typical Shaker bedroom (left) features a little cherrywood washstand, and old-fashioned clothes horse, a rope bed and a wall of built-in cupboards. The details are simple and perfect, bringing to mind William Morris's 'golden rule': 'Have nothing in your houses which you do not know to be useful or believe to be beautiful.'

CHILD SIZE

A small pine wardrobe (above) is perfectly sized for a children's bedroom. The lace cloth on top is a delicate base for a charming collection of stuffed bears, dolls and bunnies.

PATCHWORK MADE EASY

A quilt made by machine is not as complex as a hand-stitched one, but it is quick to construct and makes a handsome bedcover.

● Plan the design before you start: a pattern with a definite logic is usually more successful.

● Use no more than half a dozen different fabrics with only one or two bold colours which are repeated, in varying densities, in the fabrics.

● Cut the patches into squares, diamonds or triangles – shapes with more than four sides are very difficult to sew on a machine. Join the patches into strips then sew together.

● Interline and line the quilt, then overstitch through the three thicknesses following the outline of the patches or in a diagonal pattern across the whole quilt.

SQUARED OFF

Old card files (above) can be recycled as sophisticated toy boxes. The compartment theme is repeated in the squared shelving which is used to store and display model cars, floppy animals, sports equipment and magazines.

A machine-made patchwork quilt made of red and white cottons and shirting fabrics is a functional and good-looking cover for a child's bed.

BATHROOMS

The country bathrooms in the pictures of the French Impressionist Paul Bonnard, who painted gentle images of women bathing, usually had roll-top bath tubs on claw feet, painted tongue-and-groove walls and floors of bare wood or, occasionally, printed linoleum. Tongue-and-groove is a recurring country bathroom feature – particularly in the weatherboard cottages of North America, New Zealand and Australia – used from floor to ceiling, or for a dado, where the upper wall is either bare plaster or wallpapered.

Plaster is an excellent surface for bathroom walls. It can be painted in white, cream or pastels for a fresh look or colour-washed in stronger hues, and perhaps decorated with small handpainted panels or stencilled borders. Choose eggshell or silk finish paints; gloss is suitable for woodwork, but can cause condensation on walls.

Cream or white tiles used from floor to ceiling are the Italians' favoured treatment in a bathroom; often, instead of a bath, there is an open shower draining into an indented tilted floor. In French farmhouses, the walls and floor are often tiled too, with great decorative use being made of the dado. The room might have an upper wall and floor of white tiles studded with small green diamond shapes, a solid green dado, with cane furniture painted pink and an abundance of plants.

Many of the linoleums and vinyl sheet flooring now available are printed with traditional tiling patterns. A simple black-and-white design used with walls covered with a distressed paint finish comes straight from the ancient Roman countryside. The same room could have a turquoise green or a rusty red dado, the dado rail line painted in checkered black-and-white stripes – geometrics are as integral to the country style as floral designs are – while a pale pink and beige wall and dado is more English.

Bathroom windows usually have opaque glass and so do not need curtains. The opening can be outlined by stencilling or handpainted borders; use single colours for leaves, flowers, birds, fish or geometrics, or contrasting colours for complicated designs of two or more subjects, and frame the door with the same pattern. The upper wooden panels of the bathroom door can be replaced with plain, patterned or etched opaque glass panels or by stained glass. Sunlight shining through coloured glass is a strong country image.

Cast-iron or pressed steel tubs lined with enamel and standing on claw feet are traditional, and so are baths that

CLAW BATH
A solid roll-top enamelled bath (left) with claw feet has been sited casually on an angle in the corner of a bedroom under a sloping roof. Brass fittings and heated towel rails gleam attractively, and the sink has been set on a decorative stand.

SPACE SAVER
A narrow antique copper tub (above) is a handsome, albeit unusual, space saver. The bath has been slightly raised above ground level to show it to greater effect, and the tiles have been continued up over the edge of the platform.

are boxed in with wooden or hardboard panels; moulded plastic or acrylic panels are not appropriate, nor are coloured tubs. Separate showers look best in a cubicle of glass or its equivalent, rather than a moulded plastic unit. Sinks may be of a pedestal type, wall-mounted, built in or set into a marble-topped wash stand, and many of the traditional screw and lever tap (faucet) designs, which are widely available, are less fussy and more functional than heavy-looking contemporary versions. Like baths and sinks, toilets should be white, and a wooden seat is ideal.

Once the basics are right, it is the particulars that make a country bathroom special: a wicker chair, a duck-board or seagrass bath mat, loofahs, blue glass bottles of rose water, baskets of pretty soaps, a mirror with a painted frame, a freestanding towel rack and beautiful china soap dishes.

PAINT AND TILES
There has rightly been no attempt to restore the original blue grey paint left on a linen cupboard (below). The piece of furniture more interesting than if it had been stripped or repainted and set against clean, white tiles it looks quaint rather than shabby.

BATHING BEAUTY
The intrinsic beauty of this antique stone bath has been emphasized by partly concealing it beneath a lace canopy. At the same time an appealing private space has been created. Note the elegant light fittings and ornaments, which needn't be left out of a bathroom.

THE SPECIAL TOUCH

The rich glow of old-fashioned brass taps (above) reflects a rainbow-coloured splashback of glazed tiles. Similar colours have been used in another bathroom (right), but with very different materials.

Here, bare wood is a counterpoint to painted wood, the functional to the purely decorative. There is a witty juxtaposition of the wooden drug cabinet and the sculpture made out of a sample-size sash window complete with frame.

LETTING IN NATURAL LIGHT

Bathrooms, particularly those fitted into small apartments in converted houses, are often dark places lit only by artificial light. The country atmosphere will be emphasized if natural light is introduced by replacing the upper panels of an old wooden door with glass. Strengthened opaque glass is available plain, patterned and etched, or clear glass can be used with a muslin curtain hung behind.

● Remove the beading from one side of the door only, and lift out the wooden panel. Use the panel as a guide to the size of glass required and ask the glazier to cut two pieces to fit.
● Chose some new beading to match the original, cut it to size and mitre it at the corner.
● Place the glass in position on the door, holding it against the outside of the door with tape. Fit the beading over the glass on the inside and glue it tightly in place.

MELLOW YELLOW WARMTH
The difference between the yellows used on the painted tongue-and-groove dado and the wallpaper on the upper walls in this bathroom (top and above) is defined by a narrow understated border. The tiny fireplace is a charming feature that redefines the bathroom as a place for contemplation and relaxation as well as washing.

GARDEN ROOMS AND OUTHOUSES

SUN AND SHADE
A sheltered recess (left) provides
relief from the hot
Mediterranean sun and a perfect
place for alfresco dining. In
contrast (above), another table
has been set up in a position
chosen to catch the fullness of
the golden early evening sun.

The boundaries between inside and outside are softened in the country, and there is always a sense of continuity. The garden room – the conservatory or sunroom, the porch or balcony – is an integral part of country-style houses and emphasizes the transitional space between house and earth. There is something very nostalgic and old-fashioned about these comfortable and stylish spaces designed to take advantage of long, hot summer days with their wicker chairs and old sofas, hammocks and plants, iced tea and Henry James novels.

A garden room adds country style to the starkest modern house. It need not be a custom-made conservatory or a built-on porch: a sunny corner can be turned into a veritable paradise with garden furniture, lots of cushions, bundles of lavender and rosemary in Victorian trug baskets, green glazed pots and one or two tall, spectacular plants such as a topiary box tree or a lemon bush.

ROOMS WITH VIEWS
A yellow, green and cream tiled
floor is a distinctive feature of a
sunroom (far left) filled with
plants and cane furniture. A
canvas curtain shades the room
against the glare of the midday
sun making it a convenient
place to work as well as for
relaxing.

Looking out from a glass
conservatory (left) through the
leaves of large palms and vines
trained along the roof, the
boundary between indoors and
the outside has become confused.

CONSERVATORY FURNISHINGS

Modern conservatories
need softening with an
abundance of plants to fit
in with a country style but
compromises are necessary
if plants and humans are
to co-exist.

- The conservatory must
be well ventilated with
roof vents (vents near the
floor will cause draughts).
- Some form of shading
is necessary in summer.
- The floors must be
waterproof to stand up to
regular watering.
- Furniture must be able
to withstand humidity.
Look for types of chairs
and tables such as rattan
originally designed for use
in the tropics.
- Electric plugs should
be protected or positioned
just inside the main house.

INDOOR GARDEN ROOMS

Although there is a considerable difference in style between the conservatory and the sunroom, both are glassed-in rooms located on the sunny side of the house. Here, bathed in the sun's rays the winter can seem far away and the summer more intense and dramatic.

The conservatory, essentially a glass house associated with northern Europe and the Victorians, was originally dedicated to plants, the more exotic the better. It is a Victorian invention. The earlier equivalent is the orangery – a pavilion or loggia with open or glazed walls built in the same materials and style as the house. But Joseph Paxton's Crystal Palace, built for the 1851 Great Exhibition in London, established a vogue for elegant-looking conservatories and greenhouses made of prefabricated metal and glass.

Whether Victorian or modern in style, a large elaborate affair or not much more than a lean-to, the conservatory has a glass roof which is pitched or sloped. The deep windows are set on low walls made of the same material as the main house, or the wall is floor-to-ceiling glass. Floors

INFORMAL TRADITION

The orangery (below) – traditionally a temperate room in which citrus trees are grown – doubles as a living room and a dining area. To emphasize the informality and generous proportions of the room, the owners have opted for a combination of folding garden chairs and table, and oversized wooden furniture.

that can withstand frequent watering are traditional: they can be elegant patterns created out of coloured tiles, warm-toned brick or quarry tiles, slabs of marble, granite and slate, flagstones, even wooden decking. Floorboards left bare, painted or stencilled are durable enough if the conservatory is more living room than greenhouse.

Prefabricated conservatories, ranging from Victorian reproductions to simple mail-order versions, are widely available today in a number of sizes and styles, so it is relatively easy to find one suitable for your house and for the space available, whether it be at ground level or on a roof or balcony. They look best with the metal frame painted white; fitted with a beautiful floor, filled with plants and wicker furniture, even the plainest conservatory will be a charming addition to your house or apartment. A wooden-framed conservatory is usually more expensive and needs maintenance but it can be more in keeping with the style of the main building. Adding a sloping glass roof over a narrow path down the side of the house makes a light corridor that can be filled with plants.

In a sunroom the emphasis is less on plants and exotica. This is an unpretentious indoor space designed to take full advantage of the way the sun shines. It may be no more than a corner of a porch that has been glazed, or a room with glass all along one side. Windows may be able to be flung open or folded back to let in the breeze along with all the scents and sounds of the garden. A door might open straight on to the garden or to the porch.

If the sunroom has been built on to the house or is part of the porch, one or more of the walls may be of the same material as the exterior of the house – usually roughcast, stone, brick or weather-board; the other walls will probably be wooden. They are often painted a white or a light colour, or something altogether brighter: strong pinks or yellows, for example, that have been applied in a colourwash and consequently have a depth and lightness about them that you don't get with ordinary paint colours. Against this background, colourful floor rugs, patterned cushions and upholstery, cane and painted furniture should vie for attention among potted and hanging plants.

BLINDING LIGHT
The floor-to-ceiling windows of this upper-floor room (left) are framed in wood almost like a grid, with shelves incorporated. The orange-and-green striped blinds on the sloping roof can be opened and closed easily. Sunrooms and conservatories often become unbearably hot at the height of the summer and need to be shaded: as well as roller and Venetian blinds, softer-edged Roman ones which are drawn up in a series of wide pleats look good, as does muslin loosely draped over wires.

PORCHES

In one version or another porches or verandahs, raised slightly from ground level and covered by an open-walled roof, are used in almost every country to protect against the elements, whether a relentless sun or rain and sleet. And everywhere, bar the most extreme northern latitudes, it seems, they are regarded as open-air spots which you can enjoy as summer living rooms.

The porch is neither an indoor nor outdoor space, but provides an interval between the brightness and the heat of the outside world and the coolness and shadow of the interior. Porches overlooking the street are used as platforms from which to converse with neighbours and passers-by. Or they can be more remote, enclosed behind fences or hedges, or hidden at the side or back of the house.

The wonderful villas of the New World have verandahs built of wood with decorative barge-boarding or cast-iron. The hardwood floors are laid in planks from house to garden; often they are allowed to weather to a silvery tone. The roofs are sloped or curved, and often made out of corrugated iron, a material unfairly underrated in Europe. Alternatively the porches are solid structures of stone or brick, often built of the same materials as the walls of the house, and look rather like skirts extending the limits of the interior and drawing the onlooker into the shade.

NORWEGIAN ENTRANCE
From the front, this pretty, triple-arched Norwegian entrance porch (left) could be mistaken for an enclosed balcony – in fact, steps at the side lead up to the door concealed by the mass of flowers in front. The porch, with cut-out shapes round each arch, is one of the main decorative features of this otherwise simple house.

HEAT AND DUST
Hot climates often inspire simple architecture – this wide concrete porch (above) skirts the entire house, creating a shady outdoor living room, furnished with reclining chairs, and cooling the interior. The corrugated iron roof of a typical Australian weather-board house (left) is continued over a verandah screened at each end.

FURNITURE

CANE CHARMS

A beautiful old cane armchair (top left) takes pride of place in this sunroom, which is walled in glass and lined with a hard-wearing quarry-tiled floor.

A white cane two-seater sofa (left) with bold blue-and-white cushions adds to the freshness of an all-white porch room.

GREENERY

Conservatory furniture looks very good painted green like this armchair in a custom-built extension to the house (above).

On a raised brick platform (right) in an idyllic corner of a Spanish garden an inviting green hammock has been slung between poles.

arden rooms – whether porch or conservatory – are informal and inviting places, with furniture chosen for comfort and loosely arranged among plants in terracotta pots and wooden tubs. Sofas have loose covers made of chintz or ticking with plenty of unmatched cushions rather than tailored upholstery, are comfortable wicker designs, or are built into the porch structure and fitted with neat padded cushions. Traditional chairs include rockers and Lloyd Looms, iron-framed garden chairs, wicker and rattan. Tables are kept low and sturdy so you can rest your feet on them. Assorted sofas and chairs work well together if they are all painted one colour – white, black, red, green, or even violet. Cushions should be much in evidence, covered in flowery chintz, sailcloth and heavy woven cotton, stripes, geometrics, calico, colourful batiks or bright Hawaiian patterns.

It can get unpleasantly hot in a porch or conservatory during the middle of the day, and there needs to be some sort of shade. Blinds that can be raised and lowered easily are the best option. Heavy unbleached floor-to-ceiling linen that is allowed to swing free suits a stark porch. Bamboo and wooden Venetian blinds work well too: there is something soothing about the rhythm of wooden slats bumping against each other in a breeze. Awnings, on folding iron frames, are more common over· shops but actually make attractive shades for large domestic windows.

The final flourishes – essential ones – are provided by plants. Baskets of ferns and fuchsias hang from the roof beams, wisteria grows against the porch columns, pots of roses are grouped together, large palms are centre stage in the conservatory, white daisies and hydrangea bushes edge the entrance steps.

OUTDOOR DINING ROOMS

TRAILING VINES

A sun-washed outside dining room (below) has been created by building a low wall to separate it from the garden and a pergola overhead now entwined with vines. A mirror placed at one end increases the apparent length of space.

The pleasures of eating are even more intense when enjoyed outdoors in the heat among the smells and sounds of the garden. A simple meal of bread, good cheese and some light red wine becomes a feast when the leaves are rustling and the sun is shining through a slatted roof on the terrace. On balmy nights under a summer sky, the table is bathed in candle- and moonlight and the conversation sparkles.

Cooking food on an open fireplace or barbecue is one of the joys of outdoor living, and it saves numerous trips back and forth to the kitchen. A traditional pottery charcoal brazier or a Japanese grill is more suitable for a balcony, as well as being better looking than some of the monstrous free-standing models available; a home-made fireplace is

the ideal, however. If the dining space is a distance from the house, consider constructing a small container for an ice box in which to chill drinks.

An outdoor dining area needs some sense of enclosure; boundaries which define its limits and give it the feeling of a room. An external wall of the house, trellis, columns and plants provide some degree of shelter from the wind, as well as privacy. The roof should be open, or partially open, to the sky. It can be slatted or covered in trellis, vines or rattan blinds, all materials that can also be used to shade the 'walls' of the area. Another option is a canvas roof that looks rather like a horizontal Roman blind and is pulled open or shut with ropes. Or instead of a roof, the diners can be protected by a large canvas sun umbrella.

There is a long tradition of producing furniture especially for outdoor dining; much of it is so handsome that is has been commandeered for use inside the house. Some furniture, such as stone or marble tables and benches and low seating walls, are designed as permanent features, others with a long though limited life, like heavy teak or cast-iron tables and chairs, are intended to be left outside in all weathers. All the wicker and wood that looks so good in porches and conservatories belongs out here too but has to be moved indoors when it rains, along with folding tables and chairs. Above all, the table must be steady – not always easy on rough ground outdoors – and the chairs must be comfortable. This is a place in which to linger long after the plates have been cleared from the table.

PAVED TERRACE

A long terrace, paved with stone slabs runs the length of this stone house and is shaded by a pergola. The dining area is positioned conveniently close to the doors which lead from the kitchen out to the garden.

ROMANTIC LIGHTS

If an outdoor dining area is to have long use in the evenings, outside lighting is advisable. A more rustic atmosphere is created with candles.

● Candles on the table placed in deep glass holders to protect the flames from being extinguished by a light breeze.
● Garden flares stuck into the ground around the dining area and supplemented by candles on the table.

COUNTRY GARDENS

RIOT OF COLOUR
A solitary terracotta bird-bath
(left) has been positioned among
a mass of dahlias. For all the
apparent randomness, the hues
in this garden have been
carefully chosen and controlled
— creams, yellows, soft oranges
and pale pinks through purple
to clear red. The autumn
produce of a country garden
(above) has been collected in a
shallow basket.

The cottage garden is an untidy profusion of honeysuckles and roses, jasmines, hollyhocks, bluebells and daisies mixed with rosemary bushes and clumps of chives, against a background of evergreens. There may be a stretch of grass where you can lie in the shade of a pear tree, a tiny fountain or sundial, a shady arbour covered with rambling roses, and hedges of yew or an ancient stone wall. Paths are made of brick, flagstones or pale gravel, and somewhere in a quiet part of the garden is a seat to which you can escape unseen.

A country-style garden can be created on a balcony or flat roof. Plants can be grown in a charming assortment of wooden tubs and handsome terracotta pots. Tall palms and evergreens are useful for screening the balcony from the neighbours and provide a wind shield. Spectacular seasonal displays can include tubs and hanging baskets of pelargoniums and fuchsias, masses of irises, rambling roses and sweet peas, and a wonderful mix of herbaceous plants like lupins, campanula, poppies and peonies. A couple of dwarf apples or pear trees give blossom and fruit, French beans and tomatoes grow up canes, and herbs are nurtured in a collection of terracotta pots.

COUNTRY HERBS

A herb garden is an essential part of any country-style home. It can be as modest as a row of pots on a window-ledge provided that the position is sunny and sheltered. Essential culinary herbs are:

Basil (annual)
Bay (perennial)
Chives (perennial)
Dill (annual)
Fennel (perennial)
Marjoram (perennial)
Mint (perennial)
Parsley (biennial)
Rosemary (perennial)
Sage (perennial)
Tarragon (perennial)
Thyme (perennial)

COTTAGE GARDENS

Roses are usually regarded as a traditional feature of a cottage garden. Here (left top), rose bushes have been planted in the beds but other climbing plants – summer jasmine and clematis – have been used to cover the stone walls.

A corner sheltered by two wings of the house (left bottom) is perfect as a place to sit and a site for a garden of herbs and brightly coloured country flowers. The gravel around the edge is a labour-saving alternative to a lawn.

A grassy path (right) leads from a simple gate under a trained arch of leaves, and edges a big flower garden full of staked dahlias planted in tidy but profuse rows. On the other side of the path, a narrow bed of pink and red roses has been planted against the fence.

FLOWER GARDENS

There is much to be said for planting a winter garden, a framework of evergreens, against which to show off all the glories of herbaceous borders planted with perennials, biennials and annuals. Flowers play an essential role in the cottage garden, providing colour outside and adding a sweet-smelling timeless charm to the inside of the house: in true country style, plan to have a year-round supply of flowers and foliage growing in the garden that can be cut and used to create spectacular displays all over the house.

The lovely tangled beauty of the herbaceous borders that are associated with the country garden is emphasized if seen against an old brick or stone wall, or a rich green hedge of evergreens. Here, simple old-fashioned flowers look more appropriate than complex multi-headed hybrids. The effect should be one of happy chance, just one remove from the wild.

Spring is the time for bulbs and blossom. Tulips and irises wave their colourful heads under flowering almond and plum trees dripping with delicate garlands of bloom, and the grass is dotted with drifts of crocuses and hyacinths. Soon it is the turn of lupins, sweet-william, delphiniums, jasmine and lavender. In full summer, the choice is overwhelming, but should always include roses, some of the wonderfully romantic climbing plants such as clematis, sweet pea, passion-flower and wisteria (perhaps trained up a fruit tree), and sweet-smelling plants like pinks and carnations, night-scented stock and all sorts of herbs. In autumn, when the leaves are displaying their chameleon qualities, fuchsias and chrysanthemums are still blooming. Winter, of course, is more muted, and this is when the worth of evergreens is most evident. For colour and fragrance, the garden could include a winter sweet (Chimonanthus), a deciduous shrub with a spicy-smelling flower, one of the winter-flowering viburnums, winter-flowering honeysuckle, almost more fragrant than the summer variety, snowdrops and hellebores.

The most difficult aspect of a country-style garden, with its mass of flowers, is controlling colour. Cottage gardens can easily turn into unruly riot, but there needs to be an underlying theme to avoid jarring combinations.

One of the most successful approaches is to choose soft-hued flowers – mixing pale pinks with creamy yellows and light shades of blue, for instance – and add just one or two stronger patches of colour. One-colour gardens work well too, although usually they are not quite what they seem.

GENEROSITY OF SPIRIT
The essence of country planting is abundance, whether a moulded urn filled with delicate yellow and orange Californian poppies (left top), or an old-fashioned profusion (left bottom) in purples, blues and lilacs underscored by the silvery foliage of lamb's tongue and lavender flowers.

WATER LOVERS
A garden feature to be treasured is a stream or a pond especially if it is naturally occurring. The garden of this rambling stone cottage (above) has been densely planted with species that thrive in moist areas or in the water margins including variegated hostas, mallows, candelabra primula and bamboo.

The famous white garden at Sissinghurst in Kent, designed by Vita Sackville-West and Harold Nicolson, contains blooms that range in colour from the whitest white through cream and pale yellows to egg-yolk yellow. In a blue garden, it is much more interesting to mix whites, creams and soft yellows with the blues – which could vary from the palest shades through to violet – and perhaps use a little red for contrast.

It is easy to overlook the contribution foliage makes to the country garden. The different shapes and colours create great textural variety: for example, the tiny dark green ovate leaves of dwarf box outlining beds containing linear silvery-grey leaves of carnations, thick bright green angelica stems with large leaves, feathery blue-green dill, roses with pinnate leaves and prickly branches, the large pointed oblong leaves of the hosta, and the willow gentian's arching stems and light green tapered leaves.

The cottage garden is never formal, although it may contain a number of formal elements: for example, the beds may be laid out symmetrically and edged with dwarf box or, for a softer effect, with lavender, chives or parsley. Likewise, a parterre – a very low, maze-like symmetrical pattern usually made of dwarf box – is one of the most formal of garden features, yet planted on a small scale, perhaps using a different edging plant, and filled with annuals, it is a charming addition to a cottage garden; made of box, which is an evergreen, it has the extra advantage of looking beautiful all year round, even in winter. Topiary is associated with the formal, but belongs very much to the cottage garden. Bushes clipped into geometrical designs such as pyramids, spheres and cubes, into spirals, and into birds and animals are used as centre-pieces or in pairs to emphasize an entrance or vista.

A large, well-manicured lawn is out of place in a country-style garden, unless used for a tennis court, in which case it should be closely cut and rolled regularly. Instead, grass is more informal, restricted to several small areas, perhaps, or used for paths, although not ones that take heavy traffic. Ideally, the grassed area should be cut with an old-fashioned hand mower, which gives a rougher, more natural, finish. Grassy meadows of wild flowers look beautiful in even a tiny garden; seed mixtures of wild flowers and grass are available from specialist companies. Scented lawns of camomile or thyme require work and are not as hard-wearing as ordinary grass; however, they have a softly sculptured effect and feel interesting underfoot.

PRACTICAL PAVING

There are a number of surfaces that suit a country garden. New brick or stone paths will be softened if you grow tiny creeping plants, such as thyme or camomile, in the cracks.

- Grassy paths are obviously not as hard-wearing as those made of brick or stone, but their softness and verdant colour are good reasons for choosing them.
- Bricks – the type known as pavoirs are made for pathing – can be laid in herringbone patterns, on the diagonal, or in various forms of basketweave.
- Granite setts and gravel can be used in combination, but the gravelled part will require regular weeding. Pale gravel looks good in cottage-style gardens.
- Stone slabs are expensive but very beautiful and the most hard-wearing.

COUNTRY PRODUCE

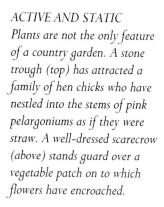

ACTIVE AND STATIC
Plants are not the only feature of a country garden. A stone trough (top) has attracted a family of hen chicks who have nestled into the stems of pink pelargoniums as if they were straw. A well-dressed scarecrow (above) stands guard over a vegetable patch on to which flowers have encroached.

APPLE CYCLE
In the summer this apple tree (right) provides much needed shade as it becomes heavy with fruit ready for picking as the leaves start to turn. During the shorter winter days its bare branches and trunk let valuable light into the nearby house although it will soon clothe itself with dense blossom.

In a flourishing vegetable garden (far right), a light cage of stakes and netting has been constructed to protect brassicas from pigeons and butterflies.

Fresh produce straight from a bountiful garden is pure country style. The ornamental qualities of many herbs and vegetables are often overlooked, but all sorts can be included in the flower garden, rather than being isolated in a kitchen garden. Edgings of chives, thyme, parsley, lavender or rosemary can replace more traditional dwarf box. Red and green cabbages, peas and beans trained up cane pyramids, and globe artichokes are just as beautiful as the espaliered and fan-trained apple and pear trees whose position of importance in the main garden is never in question.

Traditionally in larger country houses, a separate kitchen garden would be walled to keep out animals. Herbs and vegetable plants are laid to great effect in decorative beds rather than in straight rows, with pairs of currant bushes, standard gooseberries or crab apple trees – even bay trees

clipped into spheres or pyramids – at the entrance or providing a focal point. This is a labour-intensive garden and changes more frequently than a flower garden does, as crops are harvested and new vegetables replace them.

If you have room for a herb garden, it is well worth including some of the less familiar types: salad burnet and the blue-flowered borage, both of which are added to iced drinks; the delicate-flavoured chervil, one of the great culinary herbs of France, lemon balm which is often used with fish, peppery tasting savory, and lovage, which has a flavour reminiscent of celery. There are a number of less common varieties of thyme, sage, majoram and mint – mints can run rampant, so it is best to confine them in containers – that will add unusual and wonderful tastes to your meals. The delicate annuals – basil for instance – should be grown in terracotta pots on sunny window sills,

and big tubs of your favourite herbs can be placed conveniently outside the kitchen door.

Even the smallest garden has room for at least one fruit tree. Apples, peaches, plums and pears do well grafted on to dwarf stock, and they can be trained into horizontal cordons or fan shapes over supports or against walls or fences. Free-standing trees that have been allowed to grow to their full height display all the majesty of Van Gogh's peach trees, and deserve to be surrounded by a carpet of long grass. Bushes of black and red currants, gooseberries and blackberries may seem to be out of fashion, but they produce some of the loveliest bitter-sweet fruit in the garden and are well worth including, especially the standard gooseberry. Grape vines need a hot position to produce sweet fruit, but when trained over a rustic arbour or pergola, the foliage provides delicate cover for a shady seat.

THE ARCHITECTURAL ELEMENTS

Trees are as much architectural features as they are botanical ones. They add necessary height to a garden, providing various focal points, and they can act as barriers, marking the changing tempos. Trellis has a similar function, and can be deployed in highly decorative ways. Often attached to a wall to support climbers or used to screen off one part of the garden from another, trellis can also be made into low fences or arches, or to decorate the walls of a summerhouse. It has an appealing three-dimensional quality and generally looks best stained a green shade or painted white, with plants grown through it and over it.

Rustic arbours built of tree branches, pergolas made of stone columns with roofs of trellis, and iron arches and walkways covered in wonderful climbers like pillar roses, vines, wisteria, honeysuckle and clematis are as romantic as they are spectacular. Often they lead to, or cover, a perfectly placed seat hidden away in an idyllic corner of the garden. The style of garden seats has changed little over the centuries. Weathered or painted wooden ones have decorative backs or are left plain, stone benches are simple and elegant, and iron seats can be complicated lacy structures. A wooden plank set into a wall or bank, or an old railway sleeper are just as appropriate.

Garden sheds are usually relegated to a remote corner of the garden, and rightly so. But summerhouses should play a more visible role. Avoid the mass-produced versions, which are often artless and out of scale. Instead, choose a simple open shelter built on a very basic framework and embellished with trellised sides and a beautifully shaped roof. Include a built-in seat and elevate the summerhouse a little so it has a step on which you can sit in the sun.

The entrance gate frames views of the garden. It can be made of timber or iron, is either open-barred or solid, high or waist-height, and it can be simple or highly decorative, but it should always be in sympathy with the scale and style of the house. Untreated oak weathers to a light silvery colour if left unpainted. Iron is heavier and can be more decorative with bars topped with arrowheads or delicate tracery. Ideally, the walls of a country garden should be made of brick or stone, wooden palings or iron railings, rather than the pre-fabricated wooden and concrete walls commonly available today. Bamboo fencing, bought by the roll, provides a temporary disguise for an ugly wall. Other options are to paint the wall, cover it with trellis on which plants can be trained, or disguise it completely with plants.

TOOLS AND TEXTURE
The colours of the country can be vivid and brilliant or, as here, the
soft and subtle tones of faded weatherbeaten fabric or paint, mud
and stone walls, encrusted brick, and patinated metal water tanks
and watering cans.

INDEX

Page numbers in italic refer to illustrations.

ACKNOWLEDGMENTS

The publisher thanks the following photographers and organizations for their kind permission to reproduce the photographs in this book:

1 Guy Bouchet; 2 Lars Hallen; 4-5 Jean-Pierre Godeaut; 12-13 John Miller; 14 Ianthe Ruthven; 15 above Philippa Lewis/Edifice; below Lars Hallen; 16-17 S & O Mathews; 18 Yves Duronsoy; 19 above S & O Mathews; centre Christian Sarramon; below Annet Held; 20-21 Guy Bouchet; 21 below Jean-Pierre Godeaut; 22 left Yves Duronsoy; right Guy Bouchet; 23 left Annet Held; right Guy Bouchet; 24 La Maison de Marie Claire (Pataut); 24-25 Michael Freeman; 26 Christian Sarramon; 27 above left Guy Bouchet; above right Jean-Pierre Godeaut; below Yves Duronsoy; 28 above Pierre Hussenot/Agence Top (from the sculptor Cesar's house); below Yves Duronsoy; 29 Michael Freeman; 30-31 Brian Harrison/Elizabeth Whiting & Associates; 31 Jean-Paul Bonhommet; 32 Bent Rej; 33 Lars Hallen; 34 Houses & Interiors; 35 Yves Duronsoy; 36 Gilles de Chabaneix; 36-37 Lars Hallen; 37 Jean-Pierre Godeaut; 38 Spike Powell/ Elizabeth Whiting & Associates; 39 left Guy Bouchet; right Jean-Pierre Godeaut; 40 above Antoine Rozès; below Dennis Krukowski/Conran Octopus (Mary Jean and John Winkler); 41 above Fritz von der Schulenburg (Suky Schellenberg); below Yves Duronsoy; 42 Tim Street-Porter/Elizabeth Whiting & Associates; 43 Yves Duronsoy; 44-45 IPC Magazines/WPN; 45 Jean-Paul Godeaut; 46-47 Dennis Krukowski/Conran Octopus (Mary Jean and John Winkler); 47 IPC Magazines/WPN; 48-49 Paul Ryan/J B Visual Press; 50 left Michael Freeman; right Jean-Pierre Godeaut; 51 IPC Magazines/WPN; 52 Jean-Paul Bonhommet; 52-53 Ianthe Ruthven; 54 above Ianthe Ruthven (Hodgson House, Orford, New Hampshire); below Jean-Pierre Godeaut; 55 left Christian Sarramon; right Jean-Pierre Godeaut; 56 left Guy Bouchet; right Graham Henderson/Elizabeth Whiting & Associates; 57 above Paul Ryan/J B Visual Press; below Reprinted from American Design: The Farmhouse, text by Chippy Irvine, photographs by Dennis Krukowski, published by Bantam Books (c) 1987 by The Miller Press Inc; 58-59 Rene Stoeltie; 60 above Tim Street-Porter/Elizabeth Whiting & Associates, 60-61 Fritz von der Schulenburg; 61 above Di Lewis/Elizabeth Whiting & Associates; below Derry Moore; 62 above left Christian Sarramon; below left IPC Magazines/WPN; right Rene Stoeltie; 63 Di Lewis/Elizabeth Whiting & Associates; right Tim Street-Porter/Elizabeth Whiting & Associates; 64-65 Reprinted from American Design: The Farmhouse, text by Chippy Irvine, Photographs by Dennis Krukowski published by Bantam Books (c) 1987 by The Miller Press Inc; 65 Paul Ryan/J B Visual Press; 66 Michael Dunne/Elizabeth Whiting & Associates; 67 above Houses and Interiors; below Roland Beaufre/Stylograph; 68 Guy Bouchet; 68-69 IPC Magazines/WPN; 70-71 Jean-Paul Bonhommet; 72 Guy Bouchet; 73 above Simon Brown/Conran Octopus (designer Joan Lombardi Bayley); below Annet Held; 74 Fritz von der Schulenburg (Janet Fitch); 75 reprinted from American Design: The Farmhouse, text by Chippy Irvine, photographs by Dennis Krukowski published by Bantam Books (c) 1987 by The Miller Press Inc; 76 Jean-Pierre Godeaut; 77-78 Spike Powell/Elizabeth Whiting & Associates; 79 above left Spike Powell/Elizabeth Whiting & Associates; above right Gilles de Chabaneix; below Yves Duronsoy; 80 Yves Duronsoy; 80-81 Michael Freeman; 81 Fritz von der Schulenburg; 82 Richard Eastwood/Vogue Living; 83 Michael Freeman; 84 Roland Beaufre/Agence Top; 85 Guy Bouchet; 86 above left Guy Bouchet; above right Christian Sarramon; below Annet Held; 87 left Yves Duronsoy; right Rene Stoeltie; 88 IPC Magazines/WPN; 89 Houses & Interiors; 90 Pascal Hinous/Agence Top (Giverny); 90-91 Christian Sarramon; 91 Guy Bouchet; 92 above Brian Henderson/Elizabeth Whiting & Associates; below Ianthe Ruthven (Hodgson House, Orford, New Hampshire); 92-93 Annet Held; 94-95 Spike Powell/Elizabeth Whiting & Associates; 96 Rene Stoeltie; 97 Annet Held; 98 above Paul Ryan/J B Visual Press; below Jean-Pierre Godeaut; 99 Nadia MacKenzie/World of Interiors; 100 Christian Sarramon; 100-101 Lucinda Lambton/Arcaid; 101 Ianthe Ruthven (Morehouse, Tite Street, Chelsea – owner: Felix Hope-Nicholson); 102 above left Gilles de Chabaneix; above right Jean-Paul Bonhommet; below left Houses & Interiors; below right Yves Duronsoy; 103 Gilles de Chabaneix; 104 Fritz von der Schulenburg (Suki Schellenberg); 104-105 Annet Held; 105 Spike Powell/Elizabeth Whiting & Associates; 106 Peter Woloszynski/World of Interiors; 107 Jean-Pierre Godeaut; 108 above Annet Held; below Annet Held; 109 Yves Duronsoy; 110 Belle (Andrew Payne/Greg Barrett); 110-111 Ianthe Ruthven (Hodgson House, Orford, New Hampshire); 112-113 Richard Bryant/Arcaid; 114 Jean-Pierre Godeaut; 115 above Michael Freeman; below Guy Bouchet; 116-117 Jean-Pierre Godeaut; 117 Annet Held; 118 above Bill Stites/Conran Octopus (Mary Gilliatt); below IPC Magazines/WPN; 119 Ianthe Ruthven (Hodgson House, Orford, New Hampshire); 120 above Jean-Paul Bonhommet; below Bent Raj; 121 above left Richard Bryant/Arcaid; above right Fritz von der Schulenburg (Valerie Forsythe); below Houses & Interiors; 122 Houses & Interiors; 122-123 Michael Freeman; 124 left Spike Powell/Elizabeth Whiting & Associates; right Simon Brown/Conran Octopus (designer Joan Lombardi Bayley); 125 Simon Brown/Conran Octopus (designer Joan Lombardi Bayley); 126 Peter Woloszynski/World of Interiors; 127 Jean-Pierre Godeaut; 128 Paul Ryan/J B Visual Press; 129 Derry Moore; 130 Guy Bouchet; 130-131 Simon Brown/Conran Octopus (designer Joan Lombardi Bayley); 131 Houses & Interiors; 132-133 Yves Duronsoy; 133 Di Lewis/Elizabeth Whiting & Associates; 134 Yves Duronsoy; 134-135 Bent Raj; 136 La Maison de Marie Claire (Pataut/Comte); 137 Simon Brown/Conran Octopus (designer Joan Lombardi Bayley); 138 John Miller; 139 above Antoine Rozès; below Ann Kelly/Elizabeth Whiting & Associates; 140 above left J M Kolko; below left Bent Rej; right S & O Mathews; 141 Christian Sarramon; 142-143 Yves Duronsoy; 143 Jean-Pierre Godeaut; 144 Jean-Pierre Godeaut; 145 Gilles de Chabaneix; 146 above Houses & Interiors; below Yves Duronsoy; 147 Jean-Pierre Godeaut; 148 above George Wright; below S & O Mathews; 149 Andrew Lawson; 150-151 Andrew Lawson; 152 above Guy Bouchet; below Andrew Lawson; 152-153 S & O Mathews; 153 Philippe Perdereau; 154 Yves Duronsoy; 155 Heather Angel; 156-157 Jean-Pierre Godeaut (Collection Yves Leveque); 157 above left Christian Sarramon; above right Guy Bouchet; below Stephen Robson.

Pages 6-11 were specially taken for Conran Octopus by Ianthe Ruthven.

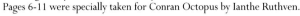